The
Perfect
Match

Other books by Dr. Kevin Leman

Making Children Mind without Losing Yours
First Time Mom
A Chicken's Guide to Talking Turkey to Your Kids about Sex
The Way of the Shepherd
Sex Begins in the Kitchen
The Birth Order Book
Sheet Music: Uncovering the Secrets of Sexual Intimacy in Marriage
When Your Best Isn't Good Enough
Women Who Try Too Hard
Becoming the Parent God Wants You to Be
Becoming a Couple of Promise
Living in a Stepfamily without Getting Stepped On
What a Difference a Daddy Makes
Making Sense of the Men in Your Life
Adolescence Isn't Terminal: It Just Feels Like It
Say Good-bye to Stress
The Real You: Becoming the Person You Want to Be
Unlocking the Secrets of Your Childhood Memories
Keeping Your Family Strong in a World Gone Wrong
Ten Secrets to Raising Sensible, Successful Kids

Forthcoming birth order books for children:

My Firstborn, There's No One Like You
My Middle Child, There's No One Like You
My Youngest, There's No One Like You
My Only Child, There's No One Like You

Audiotapes:

Why Kids Misbehave and What You Can Do about It
How to Make Your Child Feel Special
Keeping Your Family Together When the World Is Falling Apart
Living in a Stepfamily without Getting Stepped On

Videos:

Raising Successful and Confident Kids
How to Get Kids to Do What You Want

Why Kids Misbehave
Living in a Stepfamily

Video series:

Making Children Mind without Losing Yours (Christian—parenting edition)
Making Children Mind without Losing Yours (secular—public school teacher edition)
Making the Most of Marriage
Single Parenting That Works!
Bringing Peace and Harmony to the Blended Family

The
Perfect
Match

Finding & Keeping
the Love of Your Life

DR. KEVIN LEMAN

SPIRE

© 2001 by Dr. Kevin Leman

Published by Fleming H. Revell
a division of Baker Publishing Group
P.O. Box 6287, Grand Rapids, MI 49516-6287
www.bakerbooks.com

Spire edition published 2004
ISBN 0-8007-8717-X

Previously published under the title *The Birth Order Connection*

Printed in the United States of America

To my "Billsville" buddies:

To my friend, Moonhead Dietsch. His real name is Tom. We've been friends since we were three years old. We are "blood brothers." Built the same raft every summer in the creek with the invariable result—it sunk. Played all sports together, including hockey in the street. And I'm still indebted to Moon's dad and his subscription to *National Geographic*. It was Tom's and my introduction to adolescent sexual understanding of the opposite sex.

And to Wendy Winfield Dietsch. Her real name is Wendy. We've been friends since we were in kindergarten. I cried for two weeks and had to be moved to a morning class so my big sister could take me to school. Wendy still thinks I'm a big baby. Wendy was my first love in seventh grade. We danced ever so close at the "Broomstick Bounce" in October of 1956. Guess who she dumped me for? Moonhead. And what a great choice it was! Because surely they found the love of their life.

Well, I'm sure that you get the idea that these are very special people. All of our children love Tom and Wendy. And I'm so glad to report that, after almost forty years of marriage, they still very much love each other. I know you, Moonhead, with your stubborn nature, won't even read this book, but I hope you, sweet Wendy, will read a few salient parts to him. Thanks for your friendship and love.

Cub

Contents

1

How My Life Changed outside the Men's Room

I met my wife just outside the men's room at a medical center in Tucson, Arizona. I was working as a janitor at the time, and Sande was a nurse's aide. I had had my eye on this knockout brunette for a long time, but every time she passed me in the hall and said "Hi," my tongue got tied in knots and I suavely responded, "Hmrph, humph, harrumph, hi!"

Then came the day when I finally got a sentence out. Just as I was dumping a load of trash into my cart, I saw Sande walking by, so I jumped out of the men's room and said, "Would you like to go to the World's Fair with me?"

"Pardon me?" Sande asked, understandably confused. You see, the World's Fair that year was being held in Seattle, and we were in Tucson.

Surprisingly enough, even after such a bumbling introduction, Sande still agreed to have "dinner" with me—in Tucson, of course. I bought us a cheeseburger at a McDonald's and we cut it in half.

While I wouldn't recommend my method for asking a potential life mate out for a first date, I've thought a lot about how to make wise marital choices in the nearly four decades since Sande and I have been married. My work as a psychologist has led me to counsel thousands of couples, many of them considering marriage, and many others trying to keep their marriage together. One theme has become clear: If you have a rewarding and fulfilling marriage, life can throw you all kinds of curveballs (financial difficulties, sickness, child problems, etc.), and though these curveballs will pester you, they won't bury you. If your marriage is miserable, however, no amount of money, fame, fortune, or good luck can ever make you happy.

My guess is you've picked up this book because you want to figure out one of two things: Either you want help on how you can find the right person to marry, or you want to check up on the person you're with to see if maybe he or she is the right one. I'm happy to oblige.

If you're like most people, you expect to get married, have your marriage last a lifetime, and enjoy a marital relationship that fulfills your deepest emotional needs. Ideally, you'll consider your spouse to be your soul mate or kindred spirit, someone who appreciates you, remains loyal to you throughout your entire life, and understands your most intimate desires, feelings, and needs.

You want to find a person you can have an intimate connection with, with whom you don't have to be anything other than yourself. Perhaps you can even tell what he's thinking before he says it. If you were separated for three months, you'd be able to pick the conversation right back up, feeling like you didn't even miss a beat, the next time you saw him. This is the type of intimacy that leads to a soul-satisfying marriage, and it's what the vast majority of single people want and expect.

Now, don't freak out, but I've got to warn you that few people will ever experience this type of lasting relationship. In 1993, 2.3 million couples married and 1.3 million got divorced. Since many additional couples were already married, that doesn't mean half of all marriages failed in that year, but the Bureau of the Census does project that four out of ten first marriages will fail.[1] According to the National Center for Health Statistics, there are now approximately twenty million divorced people living in our country, and the median duration of any given marriage is just 7.2 years.[2] If you weed out those marriages that last but in which all the passion has died, the true number of soul-satisfying marriages—the kind we all long to have and dream about from the time we are children— is startlingly low, perhaps less than one in ten.

Don't believe me? Then take a look around you. How many married couples that you know would *you* emulate? Can you point to even ten marriages that you would characterize as happy and fulfilled? The fact is, we live in a day and age when the average oven and refrigerator have a life span that is approximately twice that of the average marriage!

What will make your marriage different? How do you plan to beat the odds? By chance? With dumb luck? Can you trust your feelings of certainty any more than the 90 percent who based their marital choice on the same thing— only to watch with frustration and pain as their fairy-tale marriage turned into a nightmare?

Finding Your True Love

As one who met his future wife while emptying a wastebasket outside a men's room, I'm not sure I'm the best person to talk about *where* to look for this life partner (though I'm certainly going to give it a shot later on), but I have a suggestion you may never have previously considered: Use birth order to help you make a wise choice. Armed with a few simple points of information, you'll be able to sort through potential partners much faster and with much more precision.

For example, suppose nineteen-year-old Sally is at a party. She's the youngest girl in a family of four children and is watching three guys talking in a corner. All of them seem interesting, and at first glance she wouldn't mind going out with any one of them, but she knows she can't get all their phone numbers without seeming a little forward, so whom should she choose?

There's Thomas, who's impeccably dressed, not a hair out of place, the epitome of grace and charm. Next to him is Bill, the fun-loving, somewhat laid-back, life-of-the-party kind of guy, his carefree attitude in total contrast to Thomas's "perfect" behavior. The third guy's name is Roger. While Roger lacks Bill's command of the stage and Thomas's style and grace, he seems like a genuinely nice, friendly guy, accommodating and polite, though less conspicuous and ambitious.

On just the information I've given you, I can tell you that, all things being equal, Sally will have the best chance of succeeding with Thomas, Roger, and Bill, in that order. After you finish reading this book, you'll understand why I'm making this suggestion; even better, you'll be able to make the same judgments for yourself.

My goal in this book is to help you use birth order to find your soul mate, the love of your life. I want you to be married to somebody who will love you like no one else ever has or ever will. I want you to enjoy a union where the two of you complement each other in unique ways and develop a wonderfully refreshing phenomenon I call "couple power"—which we'll discuss in more detail later on in this book.

But here's the key: While I can help people to a limited extent *after* they get married, the best matches are determined *before* you get married. Whom you marry *does* matter—a lot. The good news is, there are many objective criteria that will help you determine the best life mate. If you base your choice on these concrete objectives, you'll have a much better chance of enjoying a satisfying marriage than if you bet your life (quite literally) on a storm of emotion that you're sure will never end (but always does).

Though birth orders aren't foolproof, they're a great predictor and are accurate about 90 percent of the time. For example, at a church I attended some time ago, I met a widower with two young daughters. This man was absolutely terrific with his girls—gentle, affectionate, and committed. I knew right away that he was good husband material.

At the same time there was a young woman in the church whom I immediately detected would be an ideal match for this widower. Following up on my hunches, I talked to each person individually—not about each other but about their respective birth orders. The widower, I discovered, was a first born with younger sisters, while the woman was a last born with three older brothers. A perfect fit!

All I did was introduce them and then stood back and waited for the inevitable to happen. It did, and today that couple is very happily married.

Unfortunately, most young people never even think to consider the role that their birth order has played in developing their own personality, much less how it has affected their prospective spouse's personality (and how the two personalities might make it living under one roof). Instead, they're carried away by an intoxicating infatuation—drunk on love. Once the high passes, they're left to work their way through the hangover of conflicting birth orders.

Your birth order begins, of course, with the order in which you entered your family. It is further refined by the way your parents were shaped according to their birth order. Believe it or not, you'd probably have a slightly different personality if your mom had been a first born instead of a last born. Birth orders also take into account the number of siblings you have and the choices they made regarding their respective roles in life. Your personality is ultimately cemented by your own choices in responding to all of the above. In short, your birth order—as I'm using the phrase—is the totality of your family's influence on your own personality.

Think for a moment with me about the family you grew up in. I'll bet one of the members in your family (maybe it's you) is known as the "responsible" one. Somebody else is probably known as the "social" one. You might even have a "rebel."

Do you think it's a coincidence that the fun, social member is probably the last born? Does it surprise you that Billy Crystal, Whoopie Goldberg, Chevy Chase, Martin Short, Drew Carey, Jim Carrey, Steve Martin, Eddie Murphy, Goldie Hawn, Jon Stewart, Charlie Chaplin, and Jackie Gleason are *all* the youngest of their gender in their families?

Now let's flip the family over and look at the first borns. Is it mere chance that twenty-one of the first twenty-three astronauts were first borns (the other two were only children, which, technically, makes them "super" first borns)? And is it just a surprising flight of fancy that on one book tour, of the ninety-two talk-show hosts who interviewed me, only five were not first borns or onlies?

Think about it—if you're like me, you'd love to turn on your television and see Jim Carrey acting in a movie or performing a comic gig—but would you want to put that man in charge of our nation's domestic policy? Probably not. Only six presidents have been youngest born, for good reason.

The potential of any given marriage or romantic relationship is in part determined before either partner is even born. That's right. The family environment that existed before you came into this world marked you in such a way that you became largely incompatible with a certain percentage of potential marital partners, and uniquely complementary to another group of potential partners. But here's the catch—*the best marital match isn't to marry someone just like you.* For example, two first borns are likely to butt heads. Certain birth orders lend themselves to better matches. We'll discuss which ones later on. (If you married someone with the same birth order, don't despair—your marriage can work.)

Once you marry, understanding the impact of birth order can do wonders for your relationship. You'll discover why you are the way you are, but just as importantly, why your partner is the way he is. Armed with this knowledge, you can become better aware of his or her strengths and weaknesses, as well as how to love your future spouse in the way he'll feel most loved.

But What's the Point?

Okay, I know you first borns would like—right up front—a detailed, well-organized, thought-out word map to this book. You'll get an abbreviated one in just a moment, so hang on. You may also be expecting a complete annotated bibliography, a bunch of charts and graphs, and perhaps even thumb-tabs for the respective chapters. On these last points, I'm going to respond according to my own birth order: You're dreaming, buddy. Ain't gonna happen. This book was written by a random thinker, a baby of the family—but since I represent the best birth order for you to marry, you may still want to hang around for my thoughts anyway.

You babies, the youngest children, the "special ones" in the family—I know you're very anxious to get to the part where we talk about just you. In fact, some of you are probably wondering if there's a microwave popcorn gift certificate hidden in here somewhere (there's not). What you really want to know is, just how much fun will this book be? The answer is, fun enough to keep your attention. If I as a last born had to write it, you as a last born can read it! You're probably also wondering if you *really* have to read about all the other birth orders, and if perhaps it's not possible that you could read just about you. The answer to these two questions is yes and no. Yes, you need to read about the other birth orders, and no, we can't have a book just for you. You're special, but not *that* special.

And of course you middle children are probably wondering if there are going to be *any* pages devoted to you. After all, you are the least represented child in your parents' photograph books, and you always were the one who got the least attention at home. You're used to being ignored, or at least taken for granted. Well, take heart, you'll get your pages. (But not, I confess, as many as the other birth orders get! Some things never change.)

You only children, always so mature and advanced for your age, are already thinking that you've done me a great favor by allocating time in your busy schedule to read this book. In fact, books are some of your best friends, so what you really want to know is if you've met a new best friend or stumbled across another loser in life. That'll be for you to decide.

In the meantime, for the first borns and onlies, here's where we're headed. (Sorry, last borns, the editors said pictures would be too expensive, but feel free to scribble in the margins—unless of course you're reading a library book, you cheapskate.)

First, we're going to look at how birth order has shaped you and how it has shaped the person you're considering marrying, which will give you the basic information you need on how you can use birth order to make a wise marital choice. Of course, there are all kinds of exceptions to birth order and personality, so we'll discuss those as well.

Following this, I want to help you learn how to build true intimacy with your dating partner by helping you understand what makes this person tick. When we put this together with what would be the "ideal" match for you, you'll have a solid basis on which to make your choice. (Hint: Some things you'll want to have in common; in other things, you should be complete opposites—you'll find out which is which later on.)

Along the way we'll also discuss potential pitfalls in the dating world, as well as warning signs that tell you the person you're dating isn't ready for marriage, or even a serious relationship.

All right. I hope that's enough to satisfy you first borns. Any more than that and we'll lose the fun-loving last borns. Let's go!

2

Same Cub, Different Den

People frequently ask me, "How can two kids, raised by the same parents in the same household, be so different?"

The answer is simple: *It's not the same household!* The family dynamics change with the birth of each child. The home that your brothers and sisters were born into is not the same home that you were born into. Every person makes a difference, and that difference shapes who we become.

As you consider a potential life partner, you need to realize that your honey's home has molded him or her in profound ways. Her personality isn't an accident, but rather an understandable response as she sought to find her place in an already existing family. The day she was born, several roles may already have been spoken for. Of course, your partner probably didn't consciously think: "Okay, the rebel role is taken, as is the responsible Eagle Scout persona. Guess I'll have to be the clown," but unconsciously, *something very like that did happen*. Both of your birth orders will greatly impact the quality of your relationship with each other.

Let's briefly review each birth order so that you can begin to understand typical birth order characteristics.

Keep in mind, however, that there are always exceptions, which we'll deal with later in this chapter.

First Borns

First borns are natural leaders. They represent United States presidents, astronauts, and CEOs by overwhelming numbers. They frequently live with a sense of entitlement and even superiority.

However, they often come in two "flavors": compliant nurturers/caregivers (my wife, Sande) or aggressive movers and shakers. If you think about this, you can easily see how being a "caregiver" is the softer side of being the leader. Both are in control; they just use different methods.

As a rule, first borns are picky, precise people. If you walk into a bedroom, it shouldn't take you longer than five seconds to guess whether a first born or a last born decorated it. In a first born's room, everything will have its place. Even if by chance the first born tends to be a messy, he can usually find what he needs rather easily as the piles will have their own order in his mind. This attention to detail and order explains why accountants are overwhelmingly first borns—they love paying attention to small details.

Almost all the editors I have worked with are first borns, and to be honest, they can drive me nuts with their unceasingly high demand for perfection. For instance, "fair usage" in copyright laws means that you can usually quote up to one hundred words from a book without having to get written permission. I had an editor once who insisted I write to another publisher to get permission for a quote that I assumed had been under the limit.

"I thought we were okay as long as we kept it around one hundred words," I said.

"Not around," my first-born editor explained. *"Under."*

"So how many words did I quote?"

"One hundred and three."

"You mean, you actually *counted?* You really think the lawyers will sue me over three words?"

"That's the rule the lawyers have given us, Dr. Leman, and I for one am going to stick by it."

I saved myself a letter by using an ellipsis (. . .) and cutting out four words, all the while chuckling that my first-born editor had actually counted the words.

Another first-born editor had a real problem with one of my jokes. I want my books to be fun to read because, frankly, apart from being a writer, I've never been that fond of books! To me, books mean work, and I've always got something better to do than work. One of my favorite things in all the world is to walk through a hotel lobby where I've just spoken, hear somebody laugh out loud, turn, and see that she's reading one of my books. Few things give me more satisfaction than this.

"Why is this story in here?" one overly serious first-born editor wrote on the manuscript in red pencil (editors *love* red pencils).

I wrote back, "Because Dr. Leman has a sense of humor, that's why."

Yet a third editor drew my attention to the fact that I had written a run-on sentence. "How long is it?" I asked, realizing it is certainly not unheard of for a last born like me to get a bit windy.

"Let me put it this way, Dr. Leman. It begins on page 32 and ends on page 34."

"Oh," I said. "I think we can cut that."

If you marry a first born, you're going to marry someone who is likely to succeed vocationally, but you're going to have some challenges in your relationship with him. The very qualities that lead him to succeed in business work against him in regards to intimacy. Wanting to win, being competitive, taking control—these are not the attributes of a great lover, by any means.

In fact, I once met a pilot who I guessed to be a first born just by looking at him. Pilots are overwhelmingly first borns to begin with. The task is precise, leadership is important, and the ability to make quick decisions (with potentially grave consequences) fits right in with who they are. Not surprisingly, this very competent pilot (who was, indeed, a first born) admitted to me that he had just been served with divorce papers—by his third wife. He had safely landed thousands of airplanes, but he had crashed every marriage he ever entered.

A classic first born is the character Greg in the hit sit-com *Dharma and Greg*. Greg plans everything. He's conservative, successful, and neat. He even has to plan how to appear spontaneous, but you can count on him. He won't flip out, and he'll rarely do something that seems out of character.

Now, here's an important point: You won't get this person to change. He or she won't "lighten up." He may move a few degrees left or right, but it is extremely unlikely that your first-born "let's-get-it-right" guy is going to transform himself into a last-born "let's-just-have-a-good-time" guy. You need to be honest with yourself: Is this the kind of person you want to marry? Your first-born wife may not be the best at relaxing, but she'll know where everything can be found, including the car keys. Your first-born husband may be a slave to routines and predictability, but he'll probably hold down a good job.

First-Born Positives

First borns like to take charge. They are the leaders of the world who love to implement their ideas and make things happen. They are goal oriented, want complete control, and need to earn their keep. They also have a strong desire to win. In general, they tend to be very organized and are high achievers, the "Eagle Scouts" of the world. They even plan how to buy their new daily planner, and are the type of people you expect to see grow up and become astronauts, CEOs, or members of Congress. They tend to be punctual, organized, competent, and someone who wants to see things done right the first time. They also don't like surprises.

First-Born Negatives

On the negative side, first borns are often moody and occasionally lack sensitivity. They can be intimidating, particularly by pushing people too hard or refusing to take no for an answer. Sometimes they can be a bit of a "know-it-all," and often are poor delegators, in large part because they don't trust other people as much as they trust themselves. They also tend to be bossy, flaw pickers, and conscientious to a fault.

Middle Borns

To be honest, middle borns are the most difficult group to categorize, in part because they get grouped together in uncommon situations. For example, suppose there is a family of eight children. Those born into the second through seventh positions are all, technically (but not in personality), middle borns—yet all of them have widely different influences operating on them. The second-born child would feel tremendous impact from the personality of the oldest child, while the third born would be shaped in equal measure by the personalities of the first two, and so on. And then there are middle-born boys who come from families in which all the children are boys, middle-born females whose siblings are all girls, as well as middle borns who have siblings of the opposite sex.

A second-born female with an older brother may actually develop many characteristics of a first born instead of a middle born, although she is most likely to have some of both. And, of course, the same is true of a boy who was the second child born into his family, but who has an older sister.

The key to understanding middles then is to think "rebound." To avoid conflict and direct competition, a middle child will often go off in a sharply opposite direction from the child (or children) above him. For instance, if the first born is a scholastic ace who never met a course he couldn't conquer, the middle born is likely to let schoolwork slide and excel in sports, music, or vandalism. If he feels he can't compete with his older sibling(s) on an equal footing, he'll find his own route to "success," even if he is only interested in being the best at being the worst.

The "classic" middle born (if there is such a thing) is very relational, tends to be a people pleaser, and usually hates confrontation. Middle borns tend to be less driven than first borns, but much more desirous of having everybody like them—or at least be happy with them. Their basic need is to keep the oceans of life smooth, and their motto might be "Peace at any price."

Middle borns are normally good team players, reliable, steady, and loyal. There are exceptions, depending on age spacing. Sometimes a middle born will be a scrappy, ambitious climber, just aching to pull down a first born, but that's not the norm.

Middles aren't as comfortable making decisions as are first borns. They have a higher degree of doubt than first borns and consequently tend to be less gifted at solving problems (though great as mediators or when solving disputes).

One of the interesting paradoxes about middle borns is that while they tend to be mediators and negotiators, of all the birth orders they are usually the most secretive, keeping things to themselves. If you marry a middle born, be aware of this tendency toward secrecy; you're probably going to have to work hard to draw out what they're really thinking. (On the positive side, middle borns tend to have the lowest rate of infidelity of all birth orders.)

I realize that being a mediator and being secretive seems contradictory, but keep in mind that middle children are unpredictable. For their entire lives, they have played off of whatever is above and below them in the family. In fact, one of the best words to describe middle borns is *contradictory*. Though middle borns often have a "loner" streak to them, they can be very sociable in the right circumstances. At times very impatient, at other times they may be unusually laid-back. Certain life situations may turn them into an aggressive scrapper, while in other situations they play the role of the peacemaker and conflict avoider. This birth order, more than any other, is capable of jumping into a "role reversal," taking on the characteristics of a first born or last born, depending upon what is happening above or below them.

Middle-Born Positives

On the positive side, middle borns are usually very calm. They roll with the punches, are amiable, down-to-earth, and great listeners. They are skilled at seeing both sides of a problem and eager to make everybody happy. That makes them good mediators and negotiators. They can be unselfish to a fault and very loyal. These are the "nice, polite" but not intimidating class of people.

Middle-Born Negatives

On the negative side, middle borns have a difficult time setting boundaries. They can drift into becoming "co-dependents" as they try to please everybody. They also tend to avoid controversy at any cost, hate to take sides, and are not very good at making decisions that will offend others. They also tend to blame themselves when others fail.

Last Borns

The typical last born's creed is "What, me worry?" They have spent their entire lives trying to draw attention to themselves. They are often the performers, the class clowns, the life of the party. They will take far more risks than their conservative oldest siblings, but instead of con-quering the world, they usually want to enjoy it. Last borns cherish the idea of "play now, pay later." They love being pampered and spoiled and tend to crave the spotlight.

Because last borns are always learning to do for the first time what their older siblings have already accomplished (think about it—how many times can a parent get truly excited about another lost tooth? If they've already had three kids, they've had to clap for several dozen already!), they have a drive to be noticed and thus can be very good at persevering. In other words, the first "No" doesn't mean squat to a true last born. To them, "No" just means you don't agree with them—yet.

If you want to have fun, you can't find a better marital match than this. A last born is a wonderful balance to the always-serious first born, showing the oldest that life is not always deadly serious and that it's okay to have some laughs now and then.

Vocationally, last borns often choose people-oriented jobs. In fact, put together a fun-loving personality with great perseverance, and what do you have? A born salesman. Last borns could sell dead rats for a living. They can read people well, usually feel comfortable in most social situations, tend to be affectionate and uncomplicated, and as long as you notice them on a regular basis, are generally cheerful people.

As a last born, I love to make great "sales." My all-time favorite schmooze occurred rather recently. Kevin, my son, had just graduated from the Ringling School of Art and Design in Sarasota, Florida. This is a distinguished four-year art school, and I was thrilled for Kevin, though I'm still wondering where he gets his talent (I can't paint a stick).

As part of the celebration, Kevin wanted to take our family to DisneyWorld. As a former employee, Kevin had finagled some free tickets to get us in for one day. The problem came the second day. Kevin went in to see if he could find some of his buddies, but they weren't able to get us in for free.

"All right, plan B," Kevin said. "We wait outside the gate here and see if we can catch any cast members going in. They might be able to take a few of us with them."

After about an hour of waiting, my first-born wife said to me, "Why don't you just go over there and do what everybody else does?"

"What do you mean?" I asked.

"I mean, *buy some tickets!*"

"But that's not nearly as fun," I protested. I looked to my left and saw a sign that said, "Guest relations."

"Wait here," I said. "I'll be right back."

I waited in line until I was called up to the window. Not wanting to get any employee in trouble, let's just call this guy's name "Donald," as in "the Duck."

"May I help you?" Donald asked.

"Why, yes, you sure could," I said. "I'm Dr. Kevin Leman. You guys are so good to work with. We've faxed requests for tickets to you before and always received great responses, but this time, well, my son just graduated from a school down the road and he put together this trip at the last minute so we didn't have time to go through the proper channels to get complimentary tickets. Can you help me out?"

"I'd love to," Donald said, "but there's no way I can. Complimentary tickets have to be set up through the proper department."

Remember what I said about "No" not meaning squat to a last born? I looked at Donald's nametag and saw he was from Buffalo, New York, where we have our summer home.

"Hey, Donald," I said. "Check this out." I showed him my Channel 7, WKBW TV golf shirt.

"Oh," Donald said, "you're from Buffalo too."

We started talking about the Bills football team. After about five minutes, I finally said, "Well, listen, I understand you can't help me out, but do you have any ideas about what I can do?"

Now thoroughly "schmoozed," Donald said, "Actually, I'll tell you what I could do. I can walk you and your family into the park, but that means you have to stay in this park; you won't be able to go to any of the other parks."

I said, "Donald, that would be great."

In walks the manager, whom I'll call "Mickey," as in "the Mouse." I knew he was the manager because he had an earpiece in his ear. I said, "Uh-oh, everybody be on your best behavior; the boss is here."

Mickey looks up at me, clearly amused, thinking, "Who *is* this guy?"

I said, "Hey, Mickey, I bet you anything that you're the youngest son in your family, aren't you?"

I knew this because Mickey's real name is something a first born would have shortened long before. A first born goes by Susan after age twelve; the last born is forever known as Susie.

Mickey says, "Yeah, I am. How'd you know that?"

I said, "Ah, just a lucky guess. Hey, Donald, you're the first-born son, aren't you?"

Donald's jaw dropped open. His dress and attention to detail (not to mention his compulsion for obeying the rules) was a dead giveaway.

Both Mickey and Donald, and all their coworkers, stopped what they were doing and looked at me. Now I was on center stage, exactly where a last born likes to be.

"Actually," I explained, "I'm a psychologist, and I've written a book on birth orders."

The next clerk in line, a woman, leaned over and asked me, "Can you tell what I am?"

"Sure," I said. "You're a first-born daughter of two."

"That's right!"

After a few more minutes of this, Donald finally said, "Here are your tickets, Dr. Leman."

Notice, originally Donald was going to walk us in; now he's actually printing out tickets. There was a big problem, however. He printed just four.

"Oh, Donald, I didn't tell you. I've got almost my whole family here, six people total."

Now first-born Donald is stuck; a rule's a rule, and besides that, his boss is right there. Donald shot Mickey a glance that said, "What do I do?"

Last-born Mickey, no slave to rules, says, "Donald, why don't you just take care of Dr. Leman."

Donald smiled and printed out six passes—the kind where you can hop from one island to another. Not only could we get into this park, but now we could get into any of the Disney parks! These tickets are $174 each, by the way, and we got six of them!

I walked back to my first-born wife, smiling like a rooster in a henhouse, fanned the passes in front of her face, and said in a lilting voice, "Oh, well, why don't I just run over there and spend $1,200 to buy six tickets?"

Holly, my oldest born, said, "Dad, did you really get us in?"

"Not only did I get us in—we can go anywhere!"

Kevin slapped me on the back and said, "You the man, Dad! You the man!"

Sande shook her head, still not convinced there wasn't something illegal about what her last-born husband had just done.

Me? I was elated. My day was already made. "Kids, you can have any treat you want," I called out. "Today, everything's on me!"

If you can put up with the occasional embarrassment, there are certainly some fringe benefits to marrying a baby.

Last-Born Positives

If you're a last born, you're probably one of the world's cheerleaders. In all likelihood, you are probably a generally cheerful person. You have strong people skills and love to entertain and talk to others. You're the type of person who never met a stranger; you can immediately make others feel at home. You love to make people feel good or to laugh. You're an extrovert, energized by the presence of other people, and you're probably not afraid to take a risk now and then.

Last-Born Negatives

On the downside, last borns tend to get bored rather quickly. They have a strong fear of rejection and a short attention span. When the fun stops, they want to check out. They're a bit self-centered and sometimes have a bit of a Pollyannaish view of the world—that is, they're optimistic almost to a fault. This optimism may explain why last borns are so prone to get into trouble.

Because of their people skills, last borns can be pretty good manipulators. As a general rule, last borns may doom relationships more than most due to their unrealistic expectations of finding a relationship that is *always* marked by fun and sunshine—and, of course, such relationships simply do not exist for very long.

Not only are last borns the first to leave, but they are also often the first to "rush" things along. It all goes along with their compulsive nature. They may force the relationship to get it going, and then drop it as soon as it wanes.

The last-born's "lovable" exterior can unfortunately sometimes descend into a moody, mean, and aggressive temperament. To some, they may seem undisciplined, and they also have a tendency toward gullibility. In the wrong personality, the tendency toward attention-seeking can become full-blown self-centeredness.

Only Borns

The best way to describe only children is to take a first born and multiply him by two. In many ways only borns are extremely similar to first borns, but they take these traits to an extreme. Not only are they leaders, but they tend to be super perfectionists. Everything is black and white, meaning, "Do it my way or the wrong way." Because of this they tend to be critical and not a little selfish.

Only borns also live with a staunch sense of entitlement. If you marry an only child, keep in mind that you're marrying someone who has never had to share toys with siblings, compete for attention from her parents, and has always had center stage. The entire family may well have been shaped around your future spouse. While that situation creates many positive traits—confidence, leadership, and decisiveness—it also comes with the obvious difficulties. This is a person who is used to getting her own way.

More than likely, your typical only child is a list maker, a scholar, and thrives on logic. If you're hoping to ooze emotion, feeling, and affection out of this guy, frankly, you're tapping the wrong tree. He'll probably be an excellent provider. Most people will respect him. While most onlies are extremely neat, if yours isn't, he'll still know where everything is inside every pile. That's comforting. But don't expect him to be overly thoughtful, unfailingly affectionate, or romantically spontaneous. If you suggest an exotic trip to Africa, you're liable to hear about a report he read "just last week" that talks about the ten diseases you're most likely to get traveling through rain forests.

On the other hand, if you're the type of spouse who enjoys being with a big dreamer who can take a mailing list of ten people and turn it into a corporation with sales of $250 million, this is your guy. If you're a last-born male who needs a woman to bring structure and responsibility into your life—who makes sure the house is run smoothly, finances are handled wisely, and chaos is pushed back— you couldn't do better than to marry an only.

Only children also tend to be very conservative. By "conservative" I don't necessarily mean Republican; I mean they'll tend to follow the patterns established by their parents—if Mom and Dad were environmentalist activists, they'll likely be card-carrying members of Green Peace. If their parents were staunch members of the Ronald-Reagan-was-the-best-president-ever fan club, you'll probably find them at a Republican convention.

With people, only borns may be introverted. Though they enjoy one-on-one interactions, they have little patience for group "small talk" at cocktail parties.

Only-Born Positives

Only borns are the mega-movers of the world. They are task-oriented, tend to be extremely well organized, very conscientious, and ultimately dependable. They love facts, ideas, and details, and feel extremely comfortable with responsibility.

Only-Born Negatives

Only-born negatives can be tough to handle, maritally speaking. They are often unforgiving, very demanding, hate to admit they're wrong, and usually don't accept criticism well. To others, they seem very sensitive and, indeed, their feelings are easily hurt.

What If Your Birth Order Doesn't Fit?

One time, I got it wrong. Looking at Bryant Gumbel's hundred-dollar plus ties, immaculate suits, and take-charge personality, I was certain he was the first born. I had correctly pegged Katie Couric, his one-time sidekick, as a last born, but Bryant threw me off when I was told his brother Greg was the older son by three years.

"Were Greg and Bryant's parents critical?" I asked my informant.

"Very," I was told.

Bingo.

Later, I found out an additional explanation. Bryant has a personal assistant who takes care of his schedule, and his best friend, Joseph Abboud, picks out his clothing. The assistant makes sure his pens match his shirts. I bet *she's* a first born!

There are, in fact, a number of variables that can "readjust" birth order. The order of your birth is significant and long-lasting, but other factors contribute to who you are as well. We'll discuss some of these other factors in the next chapter, but in this section, I want to address birth order variables. For more detail, I suggest you read *The Birth Order Book*.

Spacing

Any gap between siblings of five years or more is significant. A third male, whose older two siblings are eight and seven years older than him, may well develop first-born tendencies, particularly if he has a younger sibling within two or three years. A family like mine, with three children, a gap of nine years, and then two more children, is almost like having two families.

Sibling Gender

The sequence of females and males is also important. For example, a quiet, reserved first-born female may have a very ambitious, first-born oriented little brother, particularly if there are other siblings who follow. My son Kevin is a middle born (number three out of five), with many middle-born qualities; but as the only male, with two younger sisters, he has adopted a few first-born characteristics. Being a first-born male is significant, even if you are actually the third or fourth child.

Physical, Mental, or Emotional Differences

I know a "split" family with five children. The first three came right after each other. Following a gap of five years, two additional girls were born within eighteen months of each other. The youngest born is very intelligent and her teachers moved her up a grade to challenge her—which put her in the same grade as her older sister. She proceeded to get better grades than her older sister and also grew in popularity, becoming a cheerleader, while her older sister hung around with the "down and outs." In this sequence, the younger "passed" the older, and took on the first-born characteristics.

Sibling Deaths, Adoptions, Illness, "Blended" Families

Depending on the age of the other children, sibling deaths, adoptions, and remarriage and divorce (resulting in "blended" families) can reshuffle traditional birth order characteristics. Protracted illness can do the same thing. Though most American presidents are first borns, Richard Nixon is an exception. But the fact that his older brother was quite sickly for a long period of time helped "push" Nixon into a different role.

Parental Birth Order

I know a last-born mom who was absolutely astonished when she visited a first-born mom. While their kids were happily playing, one of the toy's batteries went dead. The last-born mom's kids said, "Oh well, we'll find something else to play with." The first-born mom's kid looked puzzled.

"Why?" he asked.

The first-born mom went to a drawer, pulled out a special box with replacement batteries, and the kids were happily playing again in minutes. It never occurred to the last-born mom that you can buy batteries ahead of time, much less know exactly where to find them.

I can relate to the last-born mom. I think I've purchased 150,000 packages of batteries in my lifetime, but I've used no more than three. That's because I can't ever find them. And I *never* buy them until I need them.

Needless to say, different parenting styles create different personalities.

Critical Parents

One of the more toxic environments for kids is to have a critical parent. Constant criticism takes its toll. An unceasing barrage of antagonism will eventually wear down even the hardiest child, eroding the confidence of a first born or the slap-happy attitude of a last born. Criticism is like a personality flu; it can take the strongest personality and wipe that person out (especially kids).

So, if the stereotypical birth order characteristics don't seem to fit you or your love, go back through your family history and see what may have set them off. The important thing is not really whether someone is a last born or first born, but whether you know them well and are able to accept them as they are with their strengths and weaknesses.

It's also important that you learn to accept the strengths and weaknesses of your own birth order. You can improve on who you are, you can make the most of your God-given talents, but you cannot completely "remake" yourself. It is healthier to play to your strengths than to try to become something you're not.

Middle children need to be encouraged that there are many astute bosses just waiting to hire someone like you because you can see both sides of an issue really well. You're not likely to cause personality problems in an office, and overall, you tend to be a "calming influence." On the relational end, you make good marriage material. The key is to let your birth order work for you, to know all this about yourself so that when you're in a job interview or dating someone new, you can let your best light shine.

In the same vein, there is no reason to apologize for being a first born wanting all your ducks in a row. That's how you function; a clean desk is your safety net. You'll just have to ignore the last born's desk, which makes you wonder if a tornado blew through your office and left half the papers in Cleveland, Ohio, deposited on the last-born's desk. If you are married to a first born, or contemplating marrying one, there's no use trying to make him act more "laid-back." My wife absolutely cannot go to bed until the countertops in the kitchen are wiped clean, for instance.

That's really the purpose of this book: to encourage you to do your homework, get into your potential spouse's background, and ask yourself, "Is this really a good fit? Will we clash with or complement one another?"

But you still don't have all the information you need. For a complete understanding of birth order, there are several additional questions that need to be asked. Rather than looking at these questions as homework, however, consider them as the raw materials for one of the most meaningful dates you can ever have. We'll cover these in the next chapter.

3

The Most Intimate Date Imaginable

After dating your guy or gal for a while, I think it's very important that you get intimate. *Very* intimate.

More intimate than most couples ever get.

Of course, all this should be done well before you decide to get married.

Now, before you jump to conclusions, let me assure you that the intimacy I'm talking about has nothing to do with being naked or exploring each other's personal plumbing. Getting naked before you're married is a particularly good way to *block* intimacy and to hide your real self. You might know all about how your boyfriend or girlfriend likes to be touched, but anyone who has slept with them could tell you that. The intimacy I'm talking about is the type of thing that rarely gets shared today.

When I'm working with couples, I like to prescribe the "most intimate date imaginable," which actually can be a series of seven or more dates. I want these couples to discuss some deep issues that will help each partner understand who he or she really is—your motivation, your fears, your hopes, your basic understanding of life, and the rule book that you live by but may not even know exists.

Why is this important? For the simple reason that most people marry strangers and then get frustrated when they discover who they *really* married. You can live with someone for five or six years and still not know them very well. You can perform all sorts of sexual gymnastics and not have a clue about what's really inside a person. If you go over the questions I'm offering in this chapter, however, you'll have a deep understanding of who this love of your life really is—which will allow you to make a wise choice about whether this person should become your spouse.

Set aside five or six hours for this exercise. Depending on how the two of you best relate, you may even want to break this up into seven separate sessions, addressing just one question per session. Find a place where you can be alone for a long period of time and where you can talk without others listening. You might start out at a restaurant and then go out for a walk.

Bring along the following set of questions. As you and your date answer them, both of you will get an eye-opening view of why you act the way you act, and why your date is the way she is.

Question #1: How would you describe yourself as a small child between the ages of five and twelve?

I don't care whether you had red hair, braces, and skinny arms, or black hair, black teeth, and three arms. What I'm looking for are *personality characteristics.* For instance, when I asked this of one woman, she told me, "I loved books, was sort of quiet, always a good girl, never got into trouble." Right away, I knew I was dealing with a first born. Rules dominate her life. She's going to have a rigid "rule book" (more about this later) and will probably want to keep things in order.

What's the importance of this question? Well, *if you're like most people, the little boy or girl you once were, you still are*. We like to talk about how much we change, but one of the few things that psychologists and psychiatrists agree on is that our personalities are formed in the first few years of life. We are very resistant to change after that.

Once we get older, however, we often don a "mask." We confuse our "ideal" self with our "real" self and can even lose touch with who we really are. When we describe how we were as little children, however, we let our guard down. It almost feels like we're describing someone else, so we're able to be more honest and accurate.

Let's go back to the first born I mentioned just a moment ago. "As a little girl I was a good student, serious, and trustworthy—you could count on me, and teachers always did. One time, when another girl wet her pants in kindergarten, the teacher chose *me* to take her to the school office. I was reliable and conscientious, and always did what I was told to do. I wanted to be a good daughter and a model student, though I was a bit shy."

This is the type of person who would never park in a No Parking zone; her dresses will fit perfectly; her nightstand will undoubtedly have a book on it. She was like this as a little girl, and she is like that as a grown woman.

Here's the challenge: This first-born daughter will assume that everyone shares the same values and outlook on life. "How could anyone even think of parking in a No Parking zone?" she might ask her friends. If her boyfriend commits this faux pas, she might end the relationship right then and there!

The truth is, we value different things. Some of us value order, control, and discipline (typical first born). Some of us prefer fun, spontaneity, and surprise (typical last born). Others treasure getting along, being liked, and keeping the peace (typical middle). You may never have thought about what you value, but it's important that you understand who you truly are, what makes you feel comfortable, and what constitutes a "foul" in your rule book. It's equally important that you understand where your partner is coming from and what she values. As you listen to her answers, look for the clues that will unlock the door to your potential spouse's true personality.

This one question may help you understand your partner more after one conversation than you have after six months of dating. It cuts to the core of who we are and why we do what we do. Try it!

Question #2: What have you learned about women (or, if you're talking to a female, about men) while growing up?

If a guy tells you, "My mom was so weak. Dad ran right over her, and she always put up with it, covering up for him and making excuses and my sister was the same way," your caution meter should go on red alert.

By the time most boys are ten years old, they've already developed their assumptions about what women are "for." To some boys (and men), women are there to cover up men's mistakes. They see Mom helping drunk Dad avoid responsibility, taking the blame for others, acting like an unpaid housekeeper. These boys won't think twice about getting a girl pregnant and then shrugging her off with a lame excuse such as, "How do you know it's mine?" After all, they've already gotten their pleasure; now it's the woman's role to "clean up the mess."

Other boys have learned that women are to be respected, that you never raise your voice to your mom, and that males should honor and respect women by acting more refined in their presence. This is the type of young man who will take you out to dinner, open the door for you, and even pay for the meal. After you're married, he might even help you do the dishes.

It's important for you to know how your prospective husband views women or how your prospective wife views men, precisely because that's how he or she will view *you*.

I can hear some of you protesting, "But Dr. Leman, my boyfriend talks like that about his mom and sister, but he treats me very well. He buys me flowers and does all kinds of nice things."

To such a protest I respond, "Give it time." Stop having sex with this guy and see how many flowers fill your vase. Eventually, when the romance dies down, he'll view you the same way he viewed Mom and Sis.

I need to warn you about this because I counsel a number of women from good homes who assume that all men respect women. When they come across a disrespectful boyfriend, they keep making excuses for him, assuming that he can't *really* think women are inferior. If your father had a positive view of women and you expect to be treated that way by your own husband (and boys), then you better marry a man who has a positive view of women.

Take nothing for granted. Some women expect all men to be cheaters, because that's all they've ever seen men do. Some men think all women are weak, because that characteristic describes the primary females they grew up with. You need to know where your dating partner is coming from. Just because your dad had a positive view of women doesn't mean the guy you're dating does.

For you guys, it's important to understand what your future wife is expecting from her man. Does she view you as "Mr. Fix-It"? Does she assume that because you're a guy, you can't be trusted? Listen, a woman doesn't become jealous by "accident." Most often, she's responding to a dad who couldn't be trusted; when she sees you doing something entirely innocent, her mind immediately jumps to the wrong conclusion because that's all she has known when it comes to men.

The value of this question is this: By asking a prospective spouse what he thinks about men and women in general, he will be more honest by indirectly telling you what he eventually will think about *you*. Once you get this information, you have a decision to make: Has this person's view of my gender been so skewed that a long-lasting, committed relationship simply isn't possible? Or perhaps you'll discover that you are dating a person with a very healthy view of the other sex. Grade A prime marriage material!

Either way, you'll go into the marriage with your eyes wide open.

Question #3: What are three or four of your early childhood memories?

Ask your date to be as specific as she can, mentioning her age at each occurrence: "My dad took me to the state fair when I was five. He let me eat ice cream, cotton candy, and bought me a sucker, and when I spilled soda pop on my blouse, we just laughed about it. He also won me a stuffed toy by throwing darts."

Here's the key to interpreting these early childhood memories: Out of the millions of events that have occurred in your life, your brain has chosen these two or three memories. Why? Because they are consistent with how you view life.

For instance, let's consider the following three memories from a first-born woman:

Memory #1: "In the fourth grade, I remember working hard on a play that I was in. I really didn't like being in front of people, but I had a good memory so I thought I'd do okay. I spent three weeks memorizing all the lines and had them down pat, but right before my very first line in the play, I completely drew a blank. Instead of listening to my teacher—who was trying to whisper my line to me—I put my head in my hands, cried, and walked off the stage."

Memory #2: "When I was little, I built a fort behind my house. It had several rooms in it, and I loved to play in the playhouse, even if I played in it alone. On a sunny day I'd sit there and play with my dolls or read a book."

Memory #3: "When I was six years old, I got in trouble for not coming home in time for dinner. My mother had to search the neighborhood, looking for me and yelling out my name. She was furious with me, but I didn't mean to be defiant; I just lost track of time. When I finally walked in the door, I saw my father sitting down in front of his plate. He was clearly agitated and hungry, upset with me because I was late and everybody had to wait accordingly. That made me feel terrible and guilty."

This person is very rule-dominated. In her mind, there is a right way to do things, and you'd better do what you're expected to do. She's comfortable being alone, and probably a bit of a perfectionist (whenever you hear memories where people build things, it's a good sign of perfectionism).

At this point, you know you're dating a responsible first born who spends a lot of time trying to please other people—Little Miss Goody Two-Shoes. Discussing these memories will open up a window to her soul, like few other things can. You know she is afraid of breaking a rule; she's comfortable being by herself; she hates to make mistakes. If you wonder why she fell apart and started crying because

43

the birthday cake she baked for you didn't turn out exactly like she had planned, now you know. That's who she is and who she'll always be.

Now let's consider a boy's memories. See if you can guess what birth order he's from.

Memory #1: "I remember playing with my siblings and neighbor kids in our front yard when one of the kids jumped out into the middle of the street and a car had to skid on its brakes to avoid hitting him. My mom rushed out and spanked me in front of everyone, assuming it was me, even though it wasn't."

This memory is clearly focused on violating the rules. The person has a strong sense of right and wrong and of fairness. He'd make a good attorney or judge. Notice his sensitivity: "I didn't do anything wrong, yet I got in trouble." As adults, we can see how a parent would hear the screech of brakes and react, but this boy can't see the situation as a simple mistake. To him, it was an act of blatant injustice, at his expense.

Memory #2: "When my parents remodeled our home, my sister got four new walls, a new bed, a new window, all new furniture, and the carpeting color of her choice. It looked like a princess's room, with the canopy bed, pink paint, and a special hutch for her glass dolls. Me? I got one wall repaneled and a new light. That told me who mattered more."

Right away, you know you're dating a competitive person. Put him in a golf game, a swim meet, or a corporate office, and one thing is clear—this guy will want to win. He's very aware of differences and of unfair treatment. He somewhat resents the fact that girls get special treatment. Remember, this memory parallels how he sees life, and from his perspective, life is a competitive place. You have to work hard to be noticed, because basically life can be unfair.

Now, a competitive spirit can be a good thing in the workplace. There are many vocations where being competitive is essential for success. But if this guy brings his competitive nature into the marriage, he's headed for trouble. Marriage isn't about winning or losing—it's about sharing and cooperating. If you hear memories like this, you'll want to do a little more digging to make sure this guy won't be competing with you.

Memory #3: "I remember coming home from high school. My sister was baking cookies for my older brothers. I took one, and she yelled at me, saying they weren't for me. I walked away thinking, 'Why do my brothers need a dozen cookies when I can't have just one?'"

Once again, this guy's memory goes back to competition between brother and sister. Once again, he feels slighted and cheated and life seems unfair.

Overall, he sounds very much like a middle son who has first-born type qualities. He could have a critical parent and obviously feels very "stuck in the middle." Middle children often look at life on a comparison basis—they realize there's something "special" about the kid below them and something too-good-to-compete-with about the sibling(s) above them. Consequently, middles tend to define themselves by those around them.

If you marry this guy, you're going to have to work hard to make him feel appreciated. He's going to expect to be slighted and mistreated. You'll need to be wary that he doesn't bring his competitive nature into the relationship. On the other hand, if you want someone to discuss "office politics" with, who can help you decide what is right and what is wrong, this is the guy to come home to. He'll probably be a good dad, going out of his way to be fair with each of his children.

Going over these memories will tell you so much about your partner's past hurts, her fears, his anxieties, her view of life. Ask yourself, "Why did he choose this particular memory? What is that telling me? Is this the kind of person I want to spend the rest of my life with?"

Now you're *really* starting to get intimate. These questions might bring up some tension and uneasiness, but don't pull back. A soul-mate type marriage can't be built on denial and ignorance. Keep going—you've still got four more questions to explore!

Question #4: How would you describe either of your parents?

"Either" is the important word here. When I ask this question in my office, I'm particularly interested in which parent the person chooses. Whomever your date chooses first is usually the parent who impacted his life the most.

The next thing I listen for is *how* they describe their parent. For instance, when they sprinkle their conversation with words like "very" ("My mom was very polite, very social, very outgoing"), I know I'm dealing with a person who sees the world in a "black and white" manner (most probably a first born).

Next, look for the meaning behind the words. Let's say a woman tells you, "Well, I never really got to know my father. He divorced my mother when I was two, moved to Hawaii, and married another woman. He wouldn't even come to my wedding."

Even though Mom was the parent who was there and made a major positive contribution to her life, what parent do you think made the most significant impact on that daughter's life? This woman is telling you, by default, that Dad's lack of imprinting in her life has cost her big time. She might describe Mom in loving terms, but chances are Dad's negative imprint has helped screw up her relationships with the opposite sex. If she's older than thirty, my guess is she's probably already been married twice.

If you're dating this woman, I want to be honest with you. She is not a good bet. Chances are that she will do one of two things. She may be so dependent, she'll suck you dry (too clingy and too needy, looking for the dad she never had). If I'm thirty-seven and she's twenty-nine, I'm going to think, "I'm not looking to be somebody's daddy; I've got two kids already."

Conversely, her experience may lead her to marry an extremely weak man that she thinks she can control. Again, if I'm the guy she's dating, I've got to ask myself, "Do I want a woman who finds me attractive because she thinks she can control me?"

Regardless of what side this woman has fallen on, as a man you need to know that this woman has two strikes against her. Let me put this in business terms. When a company doesn't meet projected earnings in one quarter, that's forgivable; investors understand an occasional downturn. If a company acts poorly two quarters in a row, it is going to get hammered by Wall Street and the stock price is likely to plummet. When Proctor and Gamble recently announced back-to-back poor ratings, their stock price tumbled from 120 to about 55—*in one day.*

So it is with relationships. A person can overcome one or sometimes even two strikes against him. But you need to carefully evaluate whether this person's background has buried him in personality failings that will make a rewarding marriage virtually impossible. You are not "obligated" to marry anyone. If you want marital happiness, be picky and don't be shy about turning away from people who, for whatever reason, will never have the emotional maturity to be your lifelong soul mate.

Now, if you're a woman who has a history similar to the one I've just described and you want to throttle me for warning men away from you, allow me to suggest that the best thing you can do for your own sake is to know where your soft spots are and to realize your temptation to go to two basic extremes: You may find yourself wanting to marry the father you've never had, or a weak guy who will never control you. The sad truth is, neither of these guys will ultimately satisfy you. You'll feel happiest with a man who respects you and whom you respect. Guard yourself from becoming attracted to a guy for the wrong reasons. If you've had a negative father-imprinting experience, you need to train yourself to overcome your worst tendencies.

For the women reading this book, you want to look closely for any signs of disrespect. Does he describe his mom in negative ways? Does he see her as a weak woman he has learned to use and take advantage of? If so, I don't care how much money he spends on you. Eventually, he's going to treat you just like he treats Mom.

Listen for affection, one of a woman's basic needs. Is this guy affectionate toward his mom? Does he take care of her? If he does, chances are good he'll take care of you too.

While you want to pay particular attention to the parent who gets named first, go ahead and encourage your partner to describe the other parent too. Listen for the same clues. This information alone will release a ton of insight.

Question #5: What were your siblings like?

Most of us never stop to think about how much our siblings have affected us. Pop psychologists always talk about the influence of the parents (which, admittedly, is real and significant), but the fact is, we are also enormously shaped by the siblings in front of us and behind us. If you *truly* want to understand your potential soul mate, it's vital that you gain a clearer understanding of how his siblings have helped forge his personality.

For instance, let's say the first-born sister in one family turns out to be Miss Valedictorian. Chances are the second born will be the athlete. Number two has to find her own role, and taking on Miss-Straight-A's will probably seem too daunting.

Now, what happens to girl number three? Her oldest sibling, Miss Valedictorian, is the student. The next sibling became Miss All-Around-Athlete. Number three becomes the rebel. She's the one who first gets drunk, smokes weed, and breaks into a house "just for fun."

Why? Each of these young women is trying to fulfill a basic human desire: We want to be noticed. It's nothing more profound than that. You want to count, and eventually kids will do whatever they have to do to gain attention. You may not realize you've become the scholar, athlete, or rebel to gain attention—it's usually an unconscious drift—but that's what's happening inside that brain of yours.

So go ahead, put a label on each of your siblings, and encourage your partner to do the same. Other labels to consider include the saint (very religious), the business titan, the control freak, the substitute mom (or substitute dad), the adventurer, the troublemaker, the poet, the activist, the comedian, the loner. I'm sure you'll think of many others.

What you want to do is gain a better grasp of how your siblings influenced your own role in life, as well as how your partner's siblings influenced her role in life. Do you notice too much competition? Genuine affection? Estrangement? Explore each emotion.

Here are two sample families:

Family A (Dad and Mom both work long hours)
First-Born Female: Substitute Mom
Second-Born Male: The Scholar
Third-Born Male: Mr. Fix-It
Fourth-Born Male: The Saint (Mr. Religious)
Fifth-Born Female: Miss Happy-Go-Lucky

In Family A, the oldest daughter becomes the de facto mom. She gets the younger kids ready for school and watches them until her parents get home. The second-born male thus takes on many first-born characteristics. He's an excellent student, with a take-charge personality. The third becomes the type of guy who can fix anything mechanical. He can't match grades with his brother, but he can keep a car running for half a million miles. The fourth-born male is running out of roles—until he finds religion and takes it very seriously. The last-born female is the life of the party; her role is to make home a fun place to be—and keep herself on center stage.

There was an interesting episode of the hit sitcom *Everybody Loves Raymond,* in which Raymond's wife, the "good one" in her family, got the shock of her life when her formerly hippy-rebel sister announced she was becoming a nun. Suddenly, Raymond's wife's role was turned inside out. She was supposed to be the "good" child; her sister was supposed to be the "black sheep." But now her sister was becoming a nun! The psychological dissonance this created was fun to watch and true to life.

The fact is, your potential love has learned to define herself in opposition to her siblings. She did not develop her personality in a vacuum; on the contrary, she has learned to become who she is as part of a delicate interplay with her brothers and sisters. To truly understand her, you must understand how she sees herself in relation to these siblings.

> **Family B** (Dad works, Mom is a homemaker)
> First-Born Male: Mr. Eagle Scout
> Second-Born Male: The Rebel
> Third-Born Male: The Athlete
> Fourth-Born Female: Miss Girl Scout

In Family B, you have the traditional oldest male as the all-responsible Mr. Eagle Scout. He did everything right—getting on the honor roll, obeying the rules, and being respectable. This virtually guaranteed that the next boy, Mr. Rebel, would ride a motorcycle instead of a ten-speed, experiment with drugs and alcohol, and generally cause trouble. Number three comes onto the stage and realizes brother number one is already an Eagle Scout and brother number two can ride a dirt bike like nobody else, so he quits Boy Scouts, joins Little League, and becomes a star shortstop.

The fourth-born female is interesting. Though she's a last born, she's the first-born female, and her homemaking, first-born mom teaches her to cook, sew, clean, and do all sorts of "responsible" things. So instead of being the typical class clown, she takes on first-born tendencies, being *Miss* Eagle Scout (if there was such a thing). She likes to make wreaths out of dried flowers with her mom, is perfectionistic, ordered, and in control—but she still likes to be babied.

Another family phenomenon that shapes us are the "alliances" we grow up in. All families with multiple kids develop alliances. In most instances, siblings form an alliance by "skipping" over another sibling. For example, the oldest and youngest will join an alliance against the middle child. It's easier to do that psychologically, because the child who is closest to you is the one you're probably going to compete with the most.

In a typical family of four, child number one is probably going to have the closest relationship with either child number three or child number four. Three and four will probably have the most contentious relationship, as will numbers one and two. Alliances usually skip a sibling.

While you're trying to understand your love's relationship with his siblings, keep the element of alliances in mind. His problem with his sister may have more to do with birth order and alliances than with any inherent attitude toward females in general.

Question #6: What's the difference between your ideal self and your real self?

This is a question that's best answered with a piece of paper. Ask your partner to draw a line straight down the middle, and on the left side describe his ideal self—this is the self he would like to be. If your date says, "I don't get this. What am I supposed to do?" try this: "Ian, what I'm asking is this. If you overheard somebody asking a close friend of yours, 'Describe Ian to me,' what would you *hope* to hear?"

After you and Ian have completed describing your ideal selves, go to the other half of the paper and describe your real self: the person you know you are. Maybe you feel like you never quite measure up, that you're often petty, or jealous, or bitter.

Here's a sample:

Ideal Self	Real Self
Confident	Shy
Trustworthy	Absent-minded

Ideal Self	Real Self
Good sense of humor	Insecure
Unselfish	Unselfish
Caring	Caring and patient
Genuine	Occasionally hypocritical

The key here is to look at the difference between the ideal self and the real self and see if there is a huge gap. The more dissonance there is between the two, the longer you're going to want to spend getting to know this person.

What all of us should be striving for is a good self-image, that is, what you see is what you get. The gap between our ideal self and real self will hopefully get smaller and smaller as we mature. In a healthy adult, you won't find too many surprises. That's a nice place to be in life, and it's particularly nice to be married to someone like this. A lifelong marriage cries out for stability. When your kids' welfare is wrapped up in the decisions your spouse makes, you don't want that spouse to be a surprise. You want to know he or she is going to do the right thing.

This exercise will help you see what your soul mate aspires to become, giving you an opportunity to reflect on whether that's the type of person you'd like to be married to. Just as valuable, it will help you gain a clearer understanding of who he is *today*.

Question #7: How would you fill in the blank: I only matter in life when I _____?

This question will reveal the overall "theme" of your partner's life. We all have themes. For instance, a first born might say, "I only matter when I win and achieve and am in control." Babies may say, "I only matter when I get my own way, or when I get other people to do what

I want them to do. I only matter when I'm the center of attention." Middles might say, "I only matter when other people like or notice me, or when I'm able to resolve a dispute."

Most people aren't this honest. They haven't really thought about such deep inner feelings. But trying to answer this question will at least provide you with some clues.

Another reason you need to know what makes your partner feel like she matters is that if you're going to love this person for the rest of your life, you need to figure out how she wants to be loved. One of the biggest mistakes couples make is trying to treat their spouse like they'd like to be treated. That's a prescription for disaster. Don't treat your spouse like you'd like to be treated—treat her like *she* wants to be treated. And don't for an instant assume that's the same way you'd like to be loved. If you don't dig around in her past, you won't be able to really know when you're loving her or when you're being perceived as pesky.

For example, you never want to ask a first born "why?" First borns hate that question. They just want you to get in line and follow. A middle child, on the other hand, might be thrilled that someone is taking his opinion so seriously that they want an explanation.

Take the time to really get to know this person—is it someone you're truly capable of loving?

Now that you've collected all the raw data from the above seven questions, you're ready to take the next step and do something that will go a long way toward laying the foundation for a successful marriage: exchanging your rule books. In thousands of counseling sessions that I've conducted, I've discovered that one of the biggest causes of marital disputes is that couples are unaware of, and thus never exchange, their own "rule books."

Exchanging Your Rule Books

I had just finished speaking at a church in Shreveport, Louisiana, and was in a bit of a hurry to catch a plane back to Tucson. The staff from the church decided to take me out to lunch, so we climbed into the associate pastor's car and took off. I took one look at this pastor and thought, "first born." The precisely clipped hair and wrinkle-free clothes were a dead giveaway.

We pulled into the parking lot of a jam-packed Cajun restaurant. You couldn't find room to park a broomstick, much less a car. After driving around the entire parking lot once, we started going around again, and I pointed out an open space.

"There's one," I said.

The pastor looked at me like I was the devil incarnate. "I can't park there."

"Why not? It's open."

"There's a line across it."

To be honest, the pastor had a point. Clearly, this was not a legitimate parking place; it was one of those places with horizontal lines to show you that while it might be big enough to park a car in, you really shouldn't leave your car there. It's the type of marking I'd be happy to oblige *provided* there were other options and *provided* that I didn't have a plane to catch in less than two hours.

But Kevin-the-last-born Leman was hungry, we were rushed for time, and under these conditions I tend to believe that if you can fit your car anywhere on the lot, that spot *becomes* a parking place.

The first-born pastor didn't agree of course, so we made another loop of the parking lot, with no better luck.

"Oh, there's that spot again," I mentioned, but the pastor was not to be convinced. We put about 40,000 miles on his car before he became convinced that there was no other alternative.

With a huge sigh, the pastor finally took my advice and said, "I'll take a chance." Knowing his status as a first born, I wanted to say, "There's a first time for everything," but managed to hold my tongue.

Unfortunately, this poor guy had a miserable lunch. Every ten seconds, his head swiveled toward the window, where he glanced out with dread, convinced that a tow truck was going to take away his vehicle. He didn't drink the ice water, he guzzled it, but even that wasn't enough to stop him from sweating.

"You're worried, aren't you?" I asked.

"Yes, I am," he explained. "I parked illegally. I never do that."

The last-born Leman in me had to chuckle. We had gone from parking in a space with a line across it to committing a felony.

"Don't worry about it," I said. "I do it every day. In fact, my favorite place to park is in the employee of the month spot."

His eyes went wide at that one.

Each one of us walk around with a "rule book." Unfortunately, many of us are not aware of it. This guy had clearly defined parameters for parking lot etiquette. Mine are determined more by my mood than by anything so arbitrary as a yellow painted line.

While everybody has a rule book, most couples never share theirs and thus fall into many misunderstandings. Please understand me. I'm *not* suggesting that morality is relative. I wouldn't ever recommend parking in a handicapped space, for instance. The "rules" I'm talking about here are the unspoken assumptions about how people should behave in mostly morally neutral situations.

For instance, let's say a youngest-born woman marries (or is dating) a first-born man. A nice day hits, so the youngest born calls up her husband and says, "Isn't it a beautiful day out? Let's go for a walk!"

"When?" the husband asks.

"Right now! It might get overcast later."

"But I'm working!"

"But it's nice out!"

What you have here are two conflicting rule books. For the woman in this example, nice weather means getting outside, taking advantage of the sun, enjoying yourself! For the man the weather is irrelevant—he believes you never leave work in the middle of the day and that joy walking is for the weekends and weeknights.

Where most misunderstandings arise is when the partners fail to understand their own rules. Instead, they react emotionally when one of these unspoken rules is being broken. After that phone call, the wife may be frustrated, thinking, "What a dork! He worked sixty hours last week, and he can't take off one lousy afternoon? He must not love me!"

The husband, on the other hand, probably had an internal dialogue that went like this: "The nerve of that woman! Wanting me to leave work in the middle of the day! I've got two meetings, and that report has to be done by Friday. There's just no way I can do that. What does she want to do, get me fired?"

Do you see how misunderstandings become personal attacks? The woman wants to spend time with her husband, but because she's violated one of his "rules" (you never take off work in the middle of the day), he's interpreting it as her trying to get him fired!

Let's take another typical example. On Saturday morning, Barry wants to go golfing. Susan expects that they'll do yard work. Where did they get these rules? Barry's dad always went golfing on Saturdays, and Susan's dad always did yard work. Susan compares Barry to her dad and thinks he's a lazy husband, and Barry doesn't even realize he's broken a rule. He may not even know that anyone does yard work on Saturday morning—all the people he sees are at the golf course!

Yet another example happened in my own family. When my son, Kevin, graduated from art school in Florida, the entire Leman clan planned on making the trek to the Orlando area to watch our one boy flip his tassle from right to left.

My second daughter, Krissy, is married to a wonderful man named Dennis. Dennis is a schoolteacher by trade, and a principal and coach. He's a great guy, but his occupation isn't one that makes anybody rich, so he came up with the brilliant idea of letting Krissy fly out by herself so that they could save some money.

I was in the room as they discussed this and immediately realized what was going on when Krissy became unworldly silent. Dennis didn't realize how "sacred" these events are to our family. It's tough for any outsider (even though Dennis has become very much an insider) to figure out. My best friend, Moonhead, calls us the "Happy Good-Bye Family."

"Leman," he says. "It's pathetic. One of you is leaving for like, five days, and everybody stands in the driveway, waving their hands like crazy, tears running down their cheeks like somebody is going off to war. I've never seen anything like it."

Dennis didn't understand that he was violating one of Krissy's precious rules. She had never seen Sande go anywhere without me—at least, not across the country—and she couldn't understand how Dennis could even think of letting her go alone, or why he would even consider missing such a monumental (in her mind) family event.

I said to myself, *Uh oh, Dennis doesn't understand. He's trying to be nice, but Krissy isn't looking at it that way.* Even though I knew what was going on, I decided to stay out of it and kept my mouth shut.

I won't get into the details that followed, but for the record let's just say that Dennis was at Kevin's graduation.

Are you beginning to see how a woman and a man bring so much of their past into their marriage? Let me tell you, when a couple moves into their first home, they bring more than their books, CDs, and old furniture. They also bring along their mother and father, including all the dynamics of that relationship, as well as the impact of their relationship with each of their siblings. If you were a first born, your rule book may well say, "When Mom and Dad aren't around, I'm in charge!" If you're a middle child, your rule book may say, "I don't count; my older sibling gets all the responsibility, and the baby gets all the breaks." If you're the youngest, your rule book may say, "You have to treat me with extra care, because I'm the special one."

The seven questions we shared above will help you uncover your rule book and the rule book of any prospective spouse. It will show you what you expect out of life, relationships, and marriage.

If you go through this exercise before you tie the knot, you'll be better prepared than 99 percent of the couples that marry today. You'll have developed a truly intimate marriage, considering the true meaning of that word. You'll know why your partner is the way he is, why he responds the way he does, and you'll even begin to anticipate what he's thinking, feeling, and fretting about.

It is nothing less than exhilarating to know someone this well. I can't tell you how wonderful it is to watch my wife, Sande, as she's talking to someone across the room, out of earshot, while still knowing exactly what she's thinking—even though I can't hear the conversation.

Taking off your clothes doesn't develop this kind of intimacy; such closeness comes only from taking off your masks and truly sharing your hearts and lives with each other. This is the *only way* to develop the type of soul-mate intimacy that your heart desires.

4

Find Someone Who Is *Not* Compatible with You

What Makes a Match, Part 1

You're trying to watch the late-night movie, *The Tomato That Ate Tokyo,* or something equally bizarre. But it's frustrating, because every time the action gets the least bit exciting, they cut for a commercial and there *he* is again, that man wearing a plaid jacket that went out of style during your grand-father's generation. Or maybe he's wearing a clown's nose, or a hat with an alligator on it. Either way, he's shouting at the top of his voice: "Folks," he says, "come on down to Crazy Charlie's used-car lot, just next to the freeway overpass! We've got red cars, blue cars, green cars! We've got Fords, Chevrolets, and Plymouths! We've got vans, compacts, convertibles, SUVs, and pickup trucks!

"Come to Crazy Charlie's, where you get more than a car. You get fun, fun, FUN!"

In one commercial he may be riding an ostrich or a camel; in the next one he's walking on his hands or stick-ing his head in a lion's mouth. Most often he's pounding on the hood of some old wreck and telling you that you won't find a better deal anywhere in the free world.

I can't promise you this guy's cars are as good as he says they are, but I can promise you one thing: He's a last born to the nth degree! Welcome to life with the baby of the family!

Have you ever wondered what kind of woman is married to a "Crazy Charlie"? You might expect to find a platinum blonde with dark roots; a woman with a squeaky voice and enough makeup to keep Avon stock doubling every three years. Maybe you think she probably hasn't read a book since high school (assuming, that is, she actually read one then) and walks around town with forty-seven pounds of gaudy jewelry on her hands and hanging down her neck . . .

Surprise! She's probably a scholarly person who wouldn't dream of turning on the television set unless it's to watch the Public Broadcasting System. She's likely to be rather introverted and may listen to classical music. She has a few close friends but feels out of place in a crowd and hates to be conspicuous.

What I'm saying, of course, is that Mr. Flamboyant Last Born, the used-car salesman, is probably married to a prim and proper first born. What's more, if that is indeed the case, they are probably very happy together!

Is your love interest impeccably dressed while you prefer jeans and knit shirts to suits, can't wait to yank your tie off the minute you get home from work, and love weekends because you don't have to shave? Wonderful, that means you're compatible. This relationship could go somewhere.

Do you like to carefully budget out expenses, wondering whether you should go on an expensive vacation or stay home and buy a hot tub, but when you present the options to your husband he says, "Why not do both?" If so, terrific! This sounds like a wonderful match to me.

Trust me on this one. As a psychologist who has been invited into the most intimate areas of thousands of couples' lives and marriages, if you truly want to be happy, you'd better go out and look for someone who isn't at all like you.

Take the case of Todd and Shannon. Shannon is a last born to the extreme—a fun-loving woman who never let anything stand in the way of her pursuit of a good time. Occasionally, if the situation warranted it, she was known to tell a fib, although she assures me she has reformed and is doing her best to model her life after George Washington, who never told a lie, rather than Bill Clinton, who . . . well, you know what he's done!

Of course, you'd know Shannon was a last born when I told you that she made two dates for the same night. Who else but a last born would do something like that?

Well, actually she made three dates for the same night. But she had the good sense to cancel one of them.

"I knew I wasn't all that interested in going out with Aaron, but I just couldn't make up my mind between Todd and David," she explained. While I never condone lying, as a last born I could at least understand her predicament. After all, Shannon fully intended to cancel one of the dates—honest!—but in a move that can be fairly typical for a last born, she just never got around to it. As it turned out, Todd was planning to pick her up for dinner at 7:00 P.M., whereas David was planning to do the same thing at 8:30.

Finally, when Saturday rolled around and Shannon couldn't put off the inevitable any longer, she hit on what she thought was a "brilliant" idea. She called David and asked him to pick her up at 9:30. That way she'd at least be able to spend a couple of hours with Todd before asking him to take her home—hopefully, at least thirty minutes before David arrived.

Before continuing with my story, let me tell you what sort of reaction I'm getting from people who are reading this. The first borns are thinking, *Nah, he's gotta be making this up. Nobody really does that.* The last borns are smiling, thinking, "Brilliant move, Shannon! I've gotta take notes on this one!" The middle borns aren't sure yet what they think, but they'd be happy to serve as referee between David and Todd, if it would keep the peace.

Let me make one thing clear: This story is absolutely true, though the names have been changed to protect the guilty party.

As for Todd, he was a straitlaced, no-nonsense, over-achieving first born—with a master's degree in business administration from a top university and his own business (all this, and he was still in his twenties). He had met Shannon at a coffee shop, but this was to be their first "real" date.

When the evening arrived, he picked her up at 7:00 sharp, took her to his favorite restaurant, and they had a genuinely good time, up to a point. Todd loved Shannon's laugh, but he soon became annoyed at the way Shannon kept looking at her watch. She seemed preoccupied and impatient, and regardless of what Todd did to hold her attention, it was never enough.

They finished their dessert by 8:45, and Todd asked Shannon if she would like to go dancing, or perhaps take in a movie.

Immediately, the wheels started spinning inside Shannon's head. She liked Todd, she really did, but she knew she had to get back, and this was one of those rare cases when a slight fabrication might be the only way out of a tight spot.

"Oh, I'm sorry, Todd, but I really can't. A friend of mine is going through a really difficult time and I promised I'd be home to get her call later tonight and maybe go over to her house."

Todd knew she was lying, which made him feel humiliated and angry. He didn't say much as he drove her home and didn't ask to see her again, even though she assured him that she had had a wonderful time and hoped he would call her.

"I knew when I told my friend I'd be back early for her call that this might not be the best night for our first date," Shannon said, building on the lie. "But I didn't want to cancel the date either because I was afraid you wouldn't ask me out again, and I really did want to get to know you."

As soon as Todd pulled away, Shannon rushed inside the house to freshen up and get ready for her date with David—hoping that he didn't have reservations at a fancy restaurant.

Todd started to go home but had driven only a half-mile or so when he started thinking that maybe Shannon really was telling the truth. After all, even though she seemed to be in a terrible hurry, she did kiss his cheek when she said good-bye, and she made it very clear that she wanted him to call her again. Besides, there couldn't be anything wrong with giving her the benefit of the doubt.

After wrestling with the matter, he finally decided to drive back to Shannon's neighborhood, park down the street from her house, and wait for a while. Naturally he saw David arriving for his date with Shannon—so there could be no further doubt about what Shannon had really been up to and who her "friend" really was.

On the spot, Todd purposed to put Shannon out of his mind and never call her again. After all, she wasn't the sort of woman a career-oriented first born like himself ought to get involved with. She had hurt him and made him angry, and now it was time to just forget her. Forget her dancing eyes, her engaging laugh, the fun way she snuggled up to him when he said something she thought was cute, the way she played with her hair while they talked, and the way she seemed to look up to him . . .

Suddenly, Shannon's deceit made her seem more elusive, more mysterious, more inviting, and absolutely impossible to forget. Besides, corralling a girl like that would be yet another achievement that a man like Todd could add to his résumé.

Like a true first born, Todd did his research—and came up with some other disturbing facts. Shannon wasn't twenty-six as she had told him, but thirty.

"Now why would she lie about that?" Todd asked, then remembered that she had asked his age before she announced her own. When Shannon heard "twenty-eight," she might have figured he wouldn't be interested in an "older" woman. That flattered him, but then of course it also bothered him because it was another sign of her deceitfulness.

Todd, you see, wouldn't lie about anything. He was scrupulously honest about everything, even his income tax. It would never even occur to him to lie about his age, and he certainly wouldn't make two dates on the same night and lie to cover it up!

Todd became so angry he did the only thing he could think of. He called Shannon and asked for another date. When she quickly agreed, he said, "And this time I want to be your date for the entire evening. Is that okay with you?"

Shannon laughed it off. "Absolutely. Sorry about before."

"And by the way, how old did you say you are?"

"Er . . . Don't you remember?"

"Don't you *know*? It's your age after all."

Shannon laughed again. "Okay, thirty."

She laughed! Todd had caught her in a bald-faced lie, and instead of being embarrassed she just laughed! Her laid-back attitude about everything drove Todd absolutely crazy, but he couldn't help coming back for more. When they were together they had a wonderful time, and he found himself laughing more than he had in years.

Shannon promised Todd there would be no more fun and games and no more lying, but he noticed her hands were behind her back as she said this, and when he asked her if her fingers were crossed she just laughed, kissed him, and said, "Don't you trust me?"

Todd and Shannon eventually got married, and their oldest child just graduated from high school. Today, their personalities haven't changed all that much. Todd is still serious-minded, goal-oriented, and is set to retire as soon as the kids graduate from college. Shannon is fun loving, unhurried, and tends to take life as it comes (though she did, thankfully, overcome her problem with deceit).

You wouldn't have thought they were compatible nearly eighteen years ago. You still wouldn't think that they'd still be compatible today, just to consider their personalities.

So why are they so deliriously happy?

The truth is that they are a near-perfect example of a happily married couple whose personalities balance each other. If you knew nothing about birth order, you'd give them less than a 10 percent chance of making it. If you're familiar with birth order, you'd understand that they have a better chance than most at enjoying a lifelong, satisfying, and fulfilling union.

If you're still in the market for someone you haven't started dating yet, look for an opposite. The rest of this chapter will discuss some of the "opposite" things you want to consider.

Seek an Opposing Birth Order

Similar tastes in food and recreation are always nice, but I like to encourage couples to consider what truly makes a good match. If you're *too similar* in the same areas, you're likely to have more difficulty, not less, handling your disagreements.

For instance, there isn't a house on this earth that is big enough for two perfectionists. Guess what two first borns disagree on? Everything. I pity the salesman who tries to get a first-born husband and a first-born wife to agree on the same car. In fact, they probably couldn't agree on which road to take to get to the dealer! Both will have their opinions, and both will be convinced that their opinion is the only reasonable way to look at the situation.

These little disagreements can wear down a marriage real fast: how the toilet paper roll is placed (with the paper coming out on the bottom or over the top); what temperature the house should be set at; the way you roll up the toothpaste tube. Even something fun like sex can become a performance with a first born. Nothing will come easily for two first borns trying to make a go of it.

In general, similarities in birth order result in tougher matches. While first borns may fight for control, two babies will both want (and expect) to be cared for. Both have grown up feeling "special," not caring for someone else, and both—if married to each other—are going to have to get used to not taking the "special" role all the time.

Middle borns are sort of the one-size-fits-all kind of match, the universal blood donors who go with everything. They're used to blending in and make pretty good matches for first borns or babies—but again, not as good a match for fellow middle borns. Somebody has to take charge and face conflict, and in a marriage of two middles, neither is likely to assume such a role. Instead, problems get ignored, but ignoring problems never makes them go away. They just fester, get worse, and eventually result in a major eruption.

On the other hand, middles are good at seeing both sides of the issue, which makes them—on the surface, at least—a good personality for marriage. Most often, they don't expect to always get their way. Sometimes, however, this laissez-faire attitude is frustrating. I know of one elderly (first-born) man who married the classic middle-born woman. On their forty-second wedding anniversary, he asked her where she wanted to go out to eat.

"I don't care," she replied (a typical middle-born response).

Fed up with years of just this response, the controlling first born angrily retorted, "Great, we'll go to McDonald's."

She shrugged her shoulders and said, "Fine."

The first born, you understand, was looking for a fight. The fact that his middle-born wife wasn't going to give it to him made him all the more angry, so he took her through the drive-thru!

"What do you want?" he asked.

His wife remained amazingly nonplussed. "Whatever," she said.

"Get me a small fries and a coke," the first born yelled into the Golden Arches microphone.

He still didn't get his fight!

The key is to realize that every birth order has its advantages and disadvantages. If you marry a first born, you're more likely to be well cared for financially and administratively. If the first born is the provider, you probably won't have to worry about making ends meet. If the first born keeps house, it'll probably be pretty clean and organized.

On the other hand, if you're expecting your first-born husband to cuddle with you for two hours at a time, cut out from work early because the weather is nice, and take silly walks through the rain, you're probably dreaming. You're looking for a last-born son here.

Now, of course this is all generalized. As I've already explained, birth order is not entirely dependent on the order of your birth, but evolves from the family dynamics in which a person grows up. You could be a middle-born child who is seven years younger than the next sibling and who thus demonstrates first-born tendencies. You could be a last born who came along several years later and thus takes on the qualities of an only child.

You throw an alcoholic father into the mix, for instance, or a mother who suffers a severe nervous breakdown, and the whole family is going to be affected accordingly. That's why all first borns and all babies are *not* the same. Even so, talking in generalities, if you want to find a good match, find a complementary birth order.

Dr. Leman's "Best Birth Order Blends"
Only—Youngest
First Born—Youngest
Middle—Youngest

Gender plays a role here as well. If you want the absolute best match, it's a female only (or first born) marrying a male youngest child who has older sisters. The last born with older sisters is going to be the sort of person who brings out the maternal instinct in women, and the oldest sister is likely to have great maternal urges. The young man has grown up with girls who have doted on him, cared for him, and generally treated him like one of their cuddly toys. This is the same sort of treatment he is going to look for in a wife, and the best place he'll find it is with an oldest sister.

The match works on both ends. The first born, you see, needs someone to show her the pleasures of sunsets, rainbows, and to remind her that it can be fun to let her mind wander and do something crazy like go to a movie in the afternoon or make love with the lights on. The last born needs someone to show him that while having fun and daydreaming are wonderful things to do, it takes hard work and perseverance to turn those daydreams into reality.

Some of you might be surprised at the "middle—youngest" distinction. Middles are a good general match, but the reason they pair up a little bit better with the youngest is that they tend to be intimidated by the first-born's personality, whereas they aren't as likely to be intimidated by the baby's personality. Middles already have a difficult time communicating, but that difficulty grows if they're communicating with a high-powered, controlling first born.

Now let's look at some difficult pairings. See if you notice any pattern.

Dr. Leman's "Worst Birth Order Blends"
Only—Only
First—First
Youngest—Youngest
Early Middle—Early Middle
Late Middle—Late Middle

A romantic relationship between two people of the same birth order can be a lot like taking an overdose of medicine. What I mean is that most medicines have some unpleasant side effects. If you take more of a particular medicine than has been prescribed, it won't increase the benefits of the medicine, but it will increase the side effects.

The same thing happens in a marriage. Take one perfectly wonderful last born whose only vice is that he's a compulsive spender, and team him up with a financially responsible first born, and no problem. But take two perfectly wonderful last borns, who both have the same compulsive spending problem, team them up—and watch them spend their way into bankruptcy!

In a youngest—youngest blend, you're likely to have a lot of fun—and a lot of debt. Also, to be honest, I have a real concern for the children of youngest—youngest parents. It's not that I have anything against babies—I'm one myself, remember—but I know from experience how the "practical" things in life can slip our attention.

I'll never forget the time when my wife took our oldest daughter on a shopping/relaxation trip about ten years ago. I was left home with the remaining three children (our fifth, Lauren, hadn't been born yet), but the older two spent the night somewhere else, leaving me with just two-and-a-half-year-old Hannah.

Sande called me on the evening of the first full day that she had been gone, giving me the third degree drilling you'd expect from a first born. How were we getting along? What were the kids up to? It went on and on.

"Look, everything's under control, everything's okay, there's absolutely nothing to worry about," I assured her. "You need to stop worrying."

To ease Sande's mind, I told her about all the fun things we had done, the stories we read, the games we had played, et cetera. I paused at this point, waiting for Sande to say that I was the best father in the world, and how could she even think of doubting me?

Unfortunately, Sande had one more question.

"What did you feed Hannah for lunch?"

All of a sudden there was dead silence on my end of the phone.

Lunch? Er . . . I knew I'd forgotten something.

I had forgotten to feed my daughter!

Oh, I had given her breakfast—an egg and some toast—and I'd given her a bottle when I put her to bed, but nothing else the rest of the day. After all, we were so busy playing and having fun that somehow, in the rush, I simply forgot about food.

Now, imagine two people like that!

In an only—only blend, every meal will be served on time, in style, and with the exact proportion of FDA food and nutrition guidelines met on a regular basis. On the other hand, they'll butt heads so often you're liable to have a homicide!

Some of you might be surprised at why a middle—middle—two good, general matches—might not be the best for each other, but let's listen in on a conversation between two middles and I think you'll get the picture:

Mr. Harkin: "Honey, what do you feel like doing tonight? You want to take in a movie or go shopping at the mall? *(I hope you don't want to go shopping. I get bored in fifteen minutes—and those women's clothes stores! Ugh!)*

Mrs. Harkin: "Anything's fine with me. You decide." *(I'd love to go shopping, but of course, you wouldn't want to do that.)*

Mr. Harkin: "It really doesn't matter to me either. You'd probably rather go shopping, though, wouldn't you?" *(Oh, please say dinner and a movie is fine with you!)*

Mrs. Harkin: "No, really. What we do doesn't matter one way or the other to me. I just want to have a good time." *(Of course I'd rather go shopping, but I'm not going to tell you that and then see you sigh every time I mention taking the time to try on a dress. But if you take me to another Sylvester Stallone movie, I'm going to scream!)*

Mr. Harkin: "Well, I really don't mind shopping if that's what you want to do. You've been saying you need to get some new shoes." *(I can't believe I'm saying this. I hate shopping for shoes, and she has thirty-four pair sitting in her closet already! Won't I ever learn to keep my mouth shut?)*

Mrs. Harkin: "Honey, I honestly don't care." *(What am I saying? He's offered several times to go to the mall and I know that's what I really want to do. Why can't I admit it?)*

Mr. Harkin: "Well, the new Julia Roberts movie is playing at the Cineplex." *(But I've heard the new Stallone action flick is top rate!)*

Mrs. Harkin: "Sounds great to me!" *(Well, I blew it. I'll probably never get another chance to go shopping before the class reunion. But at least I won't have to sit through another blow-up-all-the-buildings movie.)*

Consider this: Both are compromising, and both are a little bit unhappy about it. They aren't getting to do what they really want to do, because they aren't willing to come out and say what they want to do. That's what often happens in a marriage of middles.

On the other hand, a male middle with older sisters and a female later born have a very good chance at success. With middles, especially, you need to consider the entire family dynamics. If you are a middle choosing a middle, it helps to be an "early" middle marrying a "late" middle (that is, one of the oldest middle children marrying one of the youngest middle children).

For instance, suppose an early middle-born's chief influence is his older brother, a hard-driving, ambitious, CEO type. Like an Arizona flash flood following the path of least resistance, the second born is going to be easy-going, relaxed, and probably otherworldly. His best marital matchup will be with a first born who has a bit of fire in her eyes. He will need someone to shake him up a bit, to help him see that you can't make it through life without showing some ambition once in a while.

If he should marry a fun-loving last born, he's headed for trouble. Their marriage will be very similar to that of two last borns, who may laugh their way to the poorhouse.

If, on the other hand, his older brother was a pleaser, someone who could never seem to do enough to win someone else's approval, the middle born is likely to be aggressive and bold, the sort of person who is going to be a "taker" rather than a "giver" and someone who doesn't have to be on the dance floor to start stepping on a few toes.

If this person marries the go-get-'em first born, we're going to experience the clash of the titans. What he needs is the fun-loving approach to life the last born can bring his way.

In general, you're looking for someone who has a different birth order than you do. The further apart you are in this regard, the better off you'll be when you come together.

Now, keep in mind, *birth orders are only indicators, not absolutes*. I am certainly not saying that two first borns should never marry each other. In fact, I have friends who are both first borns and who have been happily married for over three decades. In their case, they worked out very clear role definitions in their marriage so they're not always stepping on each other's toes.

While there are exceptions, birth orders do play a role in making us who we are, and we can use them to help us make the wisest marital choice possible. Don't let them rule you, but don't ignore them either.

There are also other factors to consider, of course, such as time spent getting to know each other, comfortableness with the opposite sex, and the sharing of common values. Let's look at each of these in turn.

Marriage Blends

First Born   **Married to First Born**   Likely high friction. Either butting heads from day one, or falling into a controller-pleaser relationship. Think John McEnroe and Tatum O'Neal, and you'll have some idea of how difficult it can be to make such a pairing work.

Married to Middle Born   The danger here is that the middle born may modify his or her own behavior to please the first-born mate. While the middle makes a good general match for anyone (except, perhaps, for another middle), she may find the first born to be somewhat intimidating and thus need drawing out.

Married to Last Born   Excellent combination. First born can teach last born how to be better organized, and that there are times when life must be taken seriously.

Middle Born   **Married to First Born**   If you marry a hard-driving first born, you may be inclined to give up your own desires and dreams to please your more dominant, first-born spouse. However, if you have some last-born tendencies, this can be a very good match for you.

Married to Middle Born   Has the potential to go either way. If one of the middle borns has first-born tendencies and one has last-born tendencies and traits, this can be a good match. On the other hand, if both partners are solid, secretive middle borns, communication is likely to suffer—though you'll do well compromising to get along and keep the peace. Has the least chance of experiencing marital infidelity.

Married to Last Born   Works best if the middle born has some first-born tendencies. If the middle is a true middle, he may find himself pulled into the last born's more irresponsible lifestyle, creating the problems seen in a last-born to last-born marriage.

Marriage Blends

Last Born	**Married to First Born** Excellent combination. The last born teaches the first born that it's okay to have fun once in a while.
	Married to Middle Born Depends on the disposition of the middle. If she has last-born tendencies, there could be trouble; if first-born tendencies, a great match.
	Married to Last Born Be careful here. You may have fun, but you'll also sometimes feel like life is getting a little out of control, with nobody in charge. Even last borns can handle controlled chaos for only so long.

Seek Someone Who Has Different Vices

Though I've never seen the movie *Natural Born Killers*, it made quite a sensation when it was released during the late nineties. Not only was it violent, but the violence was spread by a couple—a young man and young woman. It thus had sort of the Bonnie and Clyde mystique about it. We expect men to do violent, evil things—but not in the presence of women.

In no way am I suggesting that men are full of vice and women are full of nothing but "sugar and spice." As a psychologist, I've talked to women who have done some of the most evil things imaginable. You don't look at the world through rose-colored glasses when you work as a counselor.

In fact, my experience has taught me the importance of considering each other's vices before you marry. If you put two drug addicts in the same house, you're begging for trouble. If you've got two liars, two compulsive spenders, two compulsive eaters—whatever it is, two of them make the situation *ten times* worse. When you share vices, you usually end up dragging each other down and seeing your bad points multiplied.

For example, if you have a hard time sticking to a goal and your mate is the same way, how will you ever get anywhere?

If you spend money carelessly and impulsively and your mate is the same way, someday you'll be in financial trouble.

If you're disorganized and a bit sloppy and your mate is too, you may soon be buried under an avalanche of junk.

Whatever your worst vices may be, you really don't want to get married to someone who has the same shortcomings. Otherwise, you'll say, "I may drink a lot, but I don't drink as much as *her*." Or: "I know we probably can't afford to buy this dress, but Harvey just bought a boat; why should I be the only one to pinch pennies?"

Find someone who inspires you, who is strong where you are weak, and who will balance out your vices rather than multiply them.

Seek Someone Who Has Opposite Gender Siblings

What I'm about to say has nothing to do with a father's pride, but rather a psychologist's studied opinion: My son, Kevin, is going to make an absolutely wonderful catch for a young woman.

Why do I say this? He has four sisters. Psychologists realize that many marriages suffer because men don't understand women and women don't understand men. The fact is, a man likes a woman who knows how he thinks, acts, and feels, and who is comfortable in a man's presence. Women like men who don't treat them like "one of the guys." What better preparation for marriage could there possibly be for a man or woman than to grow up with several members of the opposite sex.

To a boy there is nothing quite so good, or quite so bad, as having a sister. She can be the ultimate pain in the neck, the snitch, the spoiled tagalong he can't get rid of. On the other hand, she is often one of the brightest spots of his existence, although he'd most certainly be the last one in the world to tell her so. She can be playful, creative, and fun. She can help him understand that mysterious world of pantyhose, lipstick, curling irons, and even brassieres. Whatever she is, best or worst or a combination of both, her brother does not grow up harboring many illusions and misconceptions about women.

It's also true that for a girl, the best and worst person in the world is likely to be her brother. He'll be the worst when he teases her and picks on her, sometimes so severely that he'll make her cry. She'll resent his strength when he hits her, but cherish it when he protects her from the neighborhood bully. It's often as if brothers are thinking, *Hey, I can pick on her because she's my sister, but I'd better not catch anyone else saying anything bad about her.*

If the brother is older than her, his friends will provide a "safe" crowd with which she can begin to flirt and enjoy the presence of other males. She'll hear her brother and his buddies talking about what they like and don't like about girls and thus be better prepared to face boys on her own.

The key word here is *comfortable*. In your search for a mate, look for someone who enjoys being with your gender. Notice, I didn't say enjoys having sex with your gender! I mean the type of person who has healthy cross-gender friendships and long-term platonic relationships, and who is comfortable talking with a tablefull of the opposite sex.

Jill spoke with me about how she misunderstood her husband for so long. She was the youngest born and married an oldest born—overall, a good match. While she had three sisters, she didn't have any brothers, and males always seemed like an absolute mystery to her. It took her a good five years of marriage to overcome that childhood deficit. She didn't understand her husband's interest in sex, the way he could be forceful, or the things that mattered most to him. She didn't realize that most guys would probably prefer a Hilton to a bed-and-breakfast, and that they like to be rather physical. Eventually, she got it, but this understanding came only after some time and a good bit of effort.

I've also spoken with a couple who had the opposite problem. Jim was a "man's man," five brothers and no sisters. His dad was a farmer, and he and his siblings sometimes worked fourteen hours a day. When he and Alicia got married, they bought a fixer-upper house and started to work. Jim was flabbergasted when Alicia got tired after three hours of hard yard work.

"It's not even lunch time!" he pointed out.

"Jim," Alicia tried to explain, "I started my period this morning."

"So?" he asked. "I've got allergies. You don't see me cutting out, do you?"

Jim isn't as insensitive as he sounds. Once I was able to help him realize just how taxing it can be on a woman when her period first arrives, he lightened up enormously. He just honestly did not understand women because he had never lived with a sister. As the second to youngest son of a mom who started childbearing a little later in life, he never really saw the impact of menstruation because his mom had stopped menstruating by the time he reached junior high.

This, by the way, is the perfect example of why so many issues come up *after* marriage. Alicia worked hard to cover up the effects of her period when she was dating Jim. Once they were married, however, she felt freer to share her need to slow down a little. Remember, your dating partner is always putting his or her best face forward.

Count it as a big positive if your would-be spouse has several siblings who are the same sex as you. You'll start out a few steps ahead of the other couples.

This is why you need to consider the wider dynamics of the birth order, which takes into account the gender of the siblings. With this in mind, let's look at some favorable "family dynamic blends."

> *Female first born with brothers and male last born with sisters*
>
> By now you know why this is a good match. The woman is a nurturer, comfortable with boys. The male is used to being nurtured, comfortable with older sisters.
>
> *Male first born with sisters and female last born with brothers*
>
> The same things are true of this match, only in reverse.
>
> *Female second born (with older brother) and male later born middle*
>
> The redeeming factor here is that, as the oldest girl, the female second born takes on some characteristics of the oldest first born. Since the male is a "later" middle—meaning at least the third or fourth born, he takes on some last-born characteristics, leading to a relatively good match. The same thing applies, of course, to a match between a male second born (with an older sister) and a female later born middle.

The worst family dynamic blends are these:

> *Female only and male only*
>
> This is kind of obvious, don't you think? Not only will the two butt heads, but neither will have much of a clue about the other gender.
>
> *Female last born with no brothers and male last born with no sisters*

Not only are you compounding two last borns, but neither one really knows very much about the opposite sex—at least in a psychological sense—and so wouldn't be particularly understanding and supportive of each other.

By now, you should be familiar enough with the underlying principles to map out the favorability (or unfavorability) of you and your potential spouse's birth order. There are still some additional factors that need to be considered, however. While everything we've said before talks about how you should be different (in relation to birth order), the next chapter will discuss things that you should share. Without these similarities, you're likely to face some difficult times up ahead.

5

Find Someone Who *Is* Compatible with You

What Makes a Match, Part 2

No, no, no, no, *no!* I'm not schizophrenic. At least, I wasn't the last time I analyzed myself. I realize that chapter 4 was titled "Find Someone Who *Not* Compatible with You" and that this chapter is titled "Find Someone Who *Is* Compatible with You." I can hear the first borns screaming out, "So which is it, Leman?"

My last-born's answer is "Both, naturally."

In some areas of life, diversity is a strength, pulling the two of you together. In the wrong area, however, diversity will tear you apart. There are certain things you need to share to enjoy a successful marriage.

My first aim is to get you to make full use of your brain before you march down that flower-strewn aisle. To some of you, this entire book may sound a little too "unromantic." Some people believe that when you fall in love it's something over which you have no control. You're just swept along like some poor guy riding a barrel down the Niagara River toward the falls. You know you may be in for a treacherous ride, but there's nothing you can do to stop it!

Under this scenario, a person's birth order doesn't mean anything at all. You're a captive to your love; wherever your love leads you, you must follow.

I don't believe that. After all, who decides whether to fall in love?

You do.

Who decides who to fall in love with?

Again, you do.

Put the power over your emotions back into your hands. You may be attracted to someone and decide that you want to pursue a more serious relationship. Once you get to know him or her, however, it may be a painful decision for you to decide that this person isn't right for you, but you *can* do it. You can learn to walk away.

There are two reasons why you should learn how to do this. The first is so that you will make a wise marital choice, rather than being required to "guess right" on your first attraction. The second reason is so that you learn how to rule over your emotions, protecting you from getting into an affair after you're married.

I have counseled many people who have become involved in extramarital affairs. And even though some of the "experts" will tell you that an affair can actually strengthen a marriage, I've never come across a case in which an affair left a marriage stronger or made the party involved any happier. On the contrary, an affair causes pain, guilt, and mistrust, and although a marriage can survive an affair, it takes a while for it to get back to the way it was before one of the partners broke the wedding vows.

Why, then, do people become involved in affairs? I've heard a number of different excuses. Men tell me their wives are cold and unresponsive, while women say their husbands don't talk to them or treat them with tenderness. But the one explanation that drives me up the wall, that really gets me going, is this one: "Dr. Leman, I just couldn't help myself."

This is a cousin to the equally lame, "You know, Dr. Leman, I don't really *know* how it happened. We were just good friends having a drink together, and the next thing I knew we were in bed."

"Did he slip something in your iced tea?" I ask.

"No."

"Did he conk you over the head?"

"Of course not."

"Then you chose to take your clothes off and get into that bed, didn't you?"

In a situation like this I believe both partners knew exactly where they were headed, but neither wanted to admit it because that would have "cheapened" things. It goes much easier on your conscience if you can convince yourself that it happened before you knew what hit you.

My point is this: Even though two people may be attracted to each other, they don't have to give in to that attraction. You can either give in to it, or you can fight it. If you think you'll have trouble resisting the allure, then you can figure out a way to avoid the other person, or at least avoid compromising situations.

This advice holds true for those who are married and who find themselves tempted to become involved in an affair, as well as for those who are looking for a marriage partner. You do not have to allow yourself to become involved with someone who is not good for you. You can make the conscious decision that you will only seriously consider someone who represents your best chance for true and lasting marital happiness.

In chapter 4 we discussed choosing someone who was "not compatible" with you—i.e., someone from a different birth order. In this chapter, we're going to flip that advice and look at the things that you should hold in common, beginning with common values.

Common Values

While it helps to have opposing birth orders, when it comes to values you need to look for similarity. Most fights, at root, come from a disagreement about values. The difficult thing about values is that by nature, they don't lend themselves to compromise. That's why it's so important to find someone who believes the way you do about basic truths.

Spiritual Values

I get asked all the time, "Dr. Leman, what should I do if I'm a Roman Catholic Christian and my boyfriend is a committed Orthodox Jew?"

The answer is simple: Find a new boyfriend.

I'm not one who believes in "destiny"—i.e., that out of all the billions of people in the world, your job is to find the *one* person you can be happy with. While I agree that the number of eligible partners may be smaller than most of us realize, there are certainly quite a few out there, and by all means more than one.

Because of that belief, I think that mixing faiths ultimately causes too many problems. Don't be shortsighted here. Even if one of you is willing to convert, you need to carefully consider the effect of that conversion on the extended family. Do you think it's fair to ask your boyfriend's Jewish grandmother to enter a Roman Catholic church to see her grandson get married?

If one of you doesn't convert, you need to know that dual-household faiths confuse kids. While it might sound enlightened, the fact is kids do much better with a consistent faith heritage. It simply doesn't work to celebrate Hanukkah one week and Christmas the next. If both sets of grandparents are still alive, each one will want to instruct their grandchildren. Issues like circumcision and baptism become potential battlegrounds for a new family feud.

Furthermore, for the rest of your lives you're going to struggle with extended family outings. The Jewish/Christian decision, for instance, will have a major bearing on whether the family gatherings will be held on Saturday or Sunday. Even if, with the wisdom of Solomon, you're able to come up with a compromise, there is likely to be bitterness when the grandparents seem to favor the grandkids who are brought up in their own faith.

One mother asked me to meet with her daughter. Right away, I could tell the daughter was just being respectful of her mother; she didn't really want to see me, in part because I think she knew what I would say. The daughter was from an Asian country but had become a Christian. She wanted to marry a man who was raised a Buddhist but now considered himself an atheist.

"How important is your faith to you, Anne?"

"It's the most important part of my life."

"Good. So when you have kids, what will be the most important thing you pass on to them?"

"My faith in God."

"I see. Well, let me ask you, what do you think will go through your boy's mind when he hears you talking about Jesus, and then goes fishing with his dad and asks him about this Christianity stuff, and his dad replies, 'I don't believe any of it, son'? And then when he spends time with his grandparents on your husband's side and starts talking about God, what will happen when they start talking about Buddha? What will all these conflicting messages teach him? He'll have three different worldviews placed before him. At best, he has a one-in-three chance of choosing your faith. Are you willing to take that risk?"

There was a long moment of silence. "I never thought of that," she said. "But I think my husband will become a Christian if I marry him."

"Oh, I see. How long have you been dating?"

"Two years."

"If he hasn't become a Christian to get you to marry him, why would he become a Christian when he knows he already has you as his wife?"

I could see the gears turning in her head. That bit about how she was about to make a decision that could greatly impact her kids' own religious beliefs really got to her. But in the end, Anne said, "Nevertheless, I'm going to marry him."

I never saw Anne again, but I'm willing to bet she's in a frustrating and perhaps even miserable marriage. If the most important part of her life really is her faith in God, how can she be satisfied with a husband who doesn't share what is most important to her? What kind of intimacy can she expect to have with that man? The truth is, I think she was determined to go forward because she already had the wedding planned and was too afraid of the embarrassment that might follow from calling off a wedding. It's much better to be embarrassed for a few weeks or even months than to make yourself miserable for five or six decades.

As one who has seen numerous couples try to make a relationship with contradictory spiritual values work, I'm telling you, it's not worth the effort. Even if you are able to arrive at some sort of compromise for the children's sake, you'll never be able to experience that soul-mate connection when the two of you have different worldviews. Spiritual values are too important a part of life to take for granted.

Material Values

You can disagree about what pizza to order and survive (besides, you can always order pizza with different toppings on each half). As long as you're willing to compromise, you can have a successful marriage when one person prefers watching romantic comedies and the other is a Jackie Chan action-flick fan. But if there's a wide gap in your material values—how you view and spend money—you're headed for a rocky marriage.

Especially today, when traditional values have been overturned, you can't take it for granted that your romantic interest has the same material values. Just look at how our country spends its money. For example, World Vision is one of our nation's largest relief organizations, providing food, education, and developmental help to some of the world's poorest people. Its annual income in the late nineties hovered around $600 million a year. During that same time, a single Guns and Roses hard rock tour grossed $675 million.

Think that's an isolated incident? Then tell me why the Littleton, Colorado, school district appropriated $10 million for a new athletic stadium, while parents had to raise money to repair the damage to the library that was shot up during the nation's worst school shooting in history?[1] These decisions reflect a difference in what our culture values.

Are you dating someone who would prefer to contribute to World Vision or drop $75 to attend a Guns and Roses concert (or maybe do both)? You need to know before you make a lifetime commitment.

More and more, I'm seeing couples come to me with radically different material values. Both partners assumed the other spouse felt the same way about things, and it was only after marriage that the chasm between them became so apparent.

Don't let this happen to you. Talk about these things before you get married. Does your potential wife dream of having a 6,000-square-foot home on the lake, or does she aspire to send her children to a private school? Do you envision taking vacations in Europe, or volunteering your time doing missions work in Mexico City? Will you spend Christmas in Hawaii, or visit your extended families?

These are the questions that have a major impact on married couples. Honestly ask yourself, does this woman value people more than things? Am I marrying a man who won't spend $300 to buy camping gear for the family, but who wouldn't think twice about dropping the same amount on a single titanium golf club?

I'm not asking you to pass judgment as much as I am urging you to find someone who shares the same values. Certainly, private schooling is not for everyone. Some people hate to camp. But the values that help you decide what to do are essential. If your husband expects you to work full-time and put your children in a kiddie kennel (i.e., day care) so that you can buy that second home on the ski slopes, you better make a note of that ahead of time if you would prefer to stay home.

Keep in mind, you're not just building a couple, you're building a *family*. Couples without children can sometimes stretch themselves and make compromises amongst competing material values. But if you're like most couples who eventually have kids, these issues will become very important. Compromise isn't nearly so easy then. Eventually, you're going to have to agree on many things, and it's easiest to do that before you tie the knot. If you don't agree on basic material values, compromise can become virtually impossible.

The Value of Children

Here's a sobering thought: Most people probably spend less than 10 percent of their married lives without children. Unfortunately, surprisingly few couples talk extensively about whether they want to have children, and how they'll raise the children they do have.

As soon as that first child arrives on the scene, you and your spouse are going to have a host of new issues to discuss. One couple I know were having a serious disagreement about a company-paid vacation for two to Hawaii. The husband wanted to leave their six-month-old child with a bonded, hotel-provided child care worker for two hours over the course of their five days so that the two of them could enjoy a little time alone. The wife couldn't even begin to imagine leaving her child with someone she didn't know.

"But the hotels really check these people out!" the husband protested. "Our daughter will be publicly visible at all times. And it's only for two hours!"

"I'm *not* leaving my child with an absolute stranger," the wife shot back.

This became a serious and protracted argument. Neither husband nor wife anticipated such a disagreement when they were happily dating.

The issues surrounding how you're going to raise your children will occupy much of your married life, at least until the children leave home, and even then you'll face issues regarding how active a role you want to play as grandparents. Don't take *anything* for granted. For instance, who is going to take care of your children? What kind of schooling do you plan for the children? Do you expect your spouse to coach your children's sports teams? Lead the Scout meetings? Join the PTA?

Of course, those questions assume an even deeper one—what kind of family will you have? Do you want to run six nights out of seven and have Betsy and Buford take part in constant extracurricular activities? Or do you want to make such activities rare exceptions so that the family is home together five or six nights out of seven? (Remember, you should build a home, not a hotel!)

I like to ask young marrieds—*before* they have kids—what they'd like their kids to be like. "Do you want to raise a child who cares for other people, or do you want to parent a hedonistic little sucker who has his hand out at every turn?" Invariably, of course, they answer, "We want to raise a giver." If that's so, you'll have to be different from most other families on your block. You're going to have to spend large blocks of time with your kids, and instead of shuttling them to various activities, provide them with an opportunity to give back to the family. Where else will they learn to give?

Good kids don't get that way by accident. You have to raise them that way. You have to teach them how to be responsible people. That takes time, effort, and the co-operation of both parents.

Other questions to consider include, how do the two of you view discipline? Is the man you're interested in likely to be a harsh taskmaster or an encourager? Will this woman be a good role model to your daughters, the picture of how you'd like them to turn out to be? If not, why are you marrying her? She's the person your daughter is going to see as her model woman. Dads and moms have tremendous impact on their kids; if you don't want your future kids to be just like the person you're marrying, then don't marry that person! At best, your future spouse will imprint your child in many and profound ways. At worst, he or she will become the foil against which your child chooses to rebel. Either way, your spouse's impact will be enormous.

Intelligence

Keep in mind, there are different kinds of intelligence. I have a doctorate, and the only people more surprised than me by that fact are my previous teachers! But I don't think most people who hear me talk would think of me as a stuffy intellectual. At least, I hope not!

There is book learning intelligence, commonsense intelligence, mechanical intelligence, vocational intelligence, and the like. Each form of intelligence has its place; the important thing for you to decide is which form of intelligence you most value and most want to live with for the rest of your life.

I know of some supposedly very intelligent Ph.D.s who would be hard-pressed to find a gallon of milk in a grocery store. On the other hand, I know of some high school dropouts who can put together a car engine just by "feel."

I met one bright young woman who insisted that her husband be—in her mind—*smarter* than she was. "I need to respect this man," she told me, "and it'll be hard for me to respect anyone who isn't as bright or even brighter than I am."

Her first boyfriend didn't come close to matching up, and fortunately, she ended the relationship. He was popular in school, but nowhere near her intellectual equal. While she went off to college, he stayed behind in her hometown and spent the next ten years drinking beer and dating high school cheerleaders. Eventually, the beer belly took care of the second pastime, so now he just pretty much drinks beer. She would have been bored stiff by this man within two years.

At first I was somewhat concerned because this woman was an honor student. She excelled in high school and college, even graduating *cum laude* with a four-year degree. But because she had the goal in her mind to marry someone smarter than her, she persevered and managed to find another *cum laude* graduate. Her grade point average after four years of college was 3.64. She married a man whose grade point was 3.65! Perhaps this man had no way of knowing how much one more B would have cost him!

The important thing is that she knew book intelligence was important to her, and she held back until she found someone who fit the bill.

Ambition

Do you want to marry someone who has the drive to become a United States senator, or would you be content with a guy who opened up a small shoe-repair store or barbershop? Do you want your wife to become a CEO, or do you expect her to put your vocation first?

Either choice has its benefits and drawbacks. Senators, by and large, don't have a large amount of family time. And shoe-repair storeowners aren't generally asked to be honorary chairmen of a parade.

My good friend Neil Clark Warren warns, "When spouses have different amounts of inner drive, it can cause intense frustration and conflict. But when their levels of ambition are similar, it can bond them together as they strive to reach their goals and achieve their dreams."[2]

Passion

Though I've taken a hard line on couples staying out of each other's beds until they get married, that doesn't mean I don't value the wonderful aspect of a nice bedroom romp every now and then—provided it's between husband and wife. In fact, sex is going to be a huge issue in your marriage. To my female readers, it's safe for me to say that you probably have no idea how much time your prospective husband spends thinking about sex. It is a near constant in his mind, and he's marrying you with the understanding that you will be a willing and eager participant in the marital bed. I often surprise women by telling them something that may seem harsh, but it's true to life: If you're not willing to have sex with this guy two or three times a week for the rest of your life, don't marry him. To do so is tantamount to fraud, because that's what he's expecting.

I once asked a group of men how often they thought about sex during a typical day. The average answer may surprise some of you: thirty-three. Given that most men are awake for just sixteen hours a day, this means that this group of guys averaged at least two sexual thoughts every hour.

All this means you need to have a certain passion for the person you're contemplating marriage with. While feelings alone aren't sufficient grounds to marry anyone, the total *lack* of feelings is another serious problem. If you don't want to be close to this person and hug and kiss him, then you probably lack the level of passionate attachment that is necessary for a truly satisfying marriage. Appearances aren't everything, but if you're not attracted to this person at all, you're going to run into some serious problems in your relationship.

Some readers, I suppose, will think I'm contradicting myself here when I suggest you consider sexual compatibility, especially since I strongly recommend that you not sleep together before you're married. Allow me to explain. What you don't need to do to test your sexual compatibility is to "test run" each other's bodies before marriage. Tommy Hilfiger didn't design the penis and vagina; they're custom-made for each other by no less a designer than God himself. In 99.9 percent of the couples I've worked with, the components fit just fine. Sexual fulfillment is not an issue of physical compatibility as much as it is a matter of emotional compatibility. The most important sexual organ is your brain. Trust me—you can tell how passionate a person is without seeing him or her naked.

Personally, I don't think there's anything more intimate than kissing. If you don't have the kind of passion for a person that makes you want to be close to him, affectionate with him, kiss him, and snuggle up to him, don't marry him. And if you sense that this person is reluctant to do those things with you, check out what's going on.

I urged one young man to break off a relationship for this very reason. Both he and his fiancée claimed to be very much in love, but at times she seemed almost repelled by the thought of touching him. In fact, as we talked this through, the woman confessed that she couldn't understand why he wanted to be close to her.

"All of that stuff is for after marriage, Dr. Leman, just like you said."

"But that's not what I said at all," I protested. "Sexual relations and intimate touching is clearly inappropriate, but there are healthy touches and appropriate kissing and snuggling."

When we explored this woman's background, I grew even more concerned. She had a critical and demanding father, and was so rigidly brought up that the thought of being physically close to a man freaked her out; she appeared absolutely sterile, and I saw no reason to believe this would ever change, even after marriage.

When I got the guy alone after all this stuff came out, I asked him, "How are you feeling?"

"Not very good," he confessed. "It seems unnatural and weird to have her say how much she loves me, but then not even want to touch me. I get the straight-arm if I so much as try to put my arm around her or give her a soft hug."

"Listen," I said, "you're feeling just the beginning of what you're getting yourself into if you marry this woman. She likes you all right—from a distance—and she may even be able to convince herself that she eventually will get close to you after you're married, but my experience is that women with these backgrounds will simply find a new excuse to keep you at arm's length. She'll find fault with how you get close to her or use sex as a weapon to manipulate you and punish you. It'll never end."

"Well, what do you think I should do, Dr. Leman?"

"You really want to know?"

"Yeah, I really do."

"My advice is to run. She is not good marital material until she deals with these issues."

The expression of physical intimacy in marriage is too important to play around with. To properly discuss and consider sexual compatibility, I urge every woman to pick up a copy of my book *Making Sense of the Men in Your Life*. This book will give you a good idea of just how big an issue sex is for a man. For example, as I was writing the book you're now reading, my wife of thirty-five years walked by me in her nightie. Just a glimpse of her immediately made me drop interest in everything else—including this book— and I called out, "Hey, honey, why don't you walk on over here and I'll show you what a man can do."

"No!" Sande protested. "I've got to get the kids to school on time."

School, quite frankly, was the last thought on my mind once I caught a picture of Sande in that nightie. "I'll write the note to the teacher," I explained. "I can come up with a good excuse."

"Kevin!" she said. "Not now!"

"I just can't understand why you wouldn't want to take advantage of this situation."

"Well, that's the difference between a man and a woman," Sande replied.

When I got married, I figured I'd be having sex morning, noon, and night, except that I'd have to get a job and be gone for eight hours—but in my mind, that still left me a good sixteen hours to spend wrinkling the sheets. Boy, did I find out differently, but you women need to know your husband is probably thinking the same thing.

I encourage all the men reading this book to pick up a copy of *Sex Begins in the Kitchen*. This book details the different ways that men and women become sexually aroused and fulfilled and will help you see sex from your future wife's perspective.

If you and your partner will read these two books and discuss them thoroughly, you'll have a good understanding of your sexual compatibility without running the risks posed by getting involved sexually before marriage.

Money Habits

I know I touched on this when addressing material values, but money is a big enough issue to warrant a section entirely on its own, at least from the perspective of control. Some people think money is for saving; others think it's for giving; still others think it's for spending. You need to come to some agreement here.

I know of one couple where the wife became extremely controlling in this area. She carefully budgeted every expenditure, down to the last dime. Every category of spending had its own envelope: groceries, leisure, clothes, etc. Whenever the husband spent a dollar on a pack of gum, he had to determine which envelope to take the money out of.

The marriage lasted for fifteen years before the husband finally gave up. "I feel oppressed," he admitted, "and I just can't take it anymore."

While I don't condone divorce, I understand this man's frustration. It is common for some spouses to use money as a way to carry out their emotional agenda. Often that agenda is as simple as, "I don't want this man to control me," which they achieve by turning around and controlling *him*. This woman's little envelopes were about far more than the family budget; they were her little pockets of power.

Another couple I know was extremely conservative with their money. They lived in a hot climate but had a rule that they never turned on the air conditioning before Memorial Day. Both of them worked in professional jobs and they didn't have any kids, so you wouldn't think money would be a problem—but a rule's a rule. When a friend of mine went over to their house on a particularly hot and humid day and was asked to bring a dessert, his wife unknowingly brought something that needed whipped cream on top. Wanting the dessert to be as fresh as possible, she thought she'd whip the cream right at the couple's house.

As soon as she walked in the front door she started sweating. It felt like a sauna. The day was one of Virginia's worst—hot, humid, almost oppressive. But the couple had a rule and weren't about to turn on the air conditioning. Much to my friend's surprise, he and his wife discovered that the cream simply wouldn't whip—it was too hot!

The reason this tightfisted couple was able to stay together is because both of them were equally frugal. That type of rule-setting could cause a five-alarm fire in other households, however.

Yet another example—this one also leading to divorce—occurred when a woman considered the husband's paycheck "family money" but her own paycheck (from giving horseback riding lessons) "her" money. Every time the husband wanted to buy something, he was given a lecture about how the kids needed shoes more than he needed a new fishing pole. But since the wife had her own money, she could spend it on virtually anything she wanted to. She bought new saddles, riding boots, whatever she wanted, because that was "her" money.

Once again, these are the attitudes that destroy affection faster than you can imagine. Take the time to talk this issue over, and then watch your partner very closely to see what role money plays in his life.

Flexibility

This is one trait suggested to me by Dr. Neil Clark Warren. Regardless of how much care you use in choosing a marital partner, certain differences are going to arise. What I have seen over the years, however, is that the same problems that cause some couples to fight incessantly are quickly resolved by other couples.

What is the difference? Nine times out of ten, it is flexibility.

Neil writes about a couple where the husband wants privacy while the wife wants intimacy. The husband is a night owl and the wife is an early bird. The wife wants three meals at traditional times; the husband is content to grab a cup of coffee for breakfast, pick up a snack in the afternoon, and then have a really big meal late in the evening. One partner loves to talk; the other is reticent. Nevertheless, these two had a very rewarding and satisfying marriage. How'd they do it? I'll let Neil tell you.

> As they began to recognize the kind of fix they were in, they started to think about ways to deal with it. They began to mobilize their adaptive resources. [Both said] that if they had not both grown up in large families where they had to be flexible, their marriage would not have lasted. There were many times, they said, when their differences hurt and frustrated them, when they became angry and made threats of all kinds. These times would have killed their love if they had not used their abilities to adjust.
>
> Being flexible instead of unbending, adaptive instead of rigid, can save a couple's marriage from being destroyed by differ-

ences. Of course, it takes *two* people willing to compromise and adjust. When one partner bends and flexes every time, the relationship becomes unbalanced and "out of whack."[3]

The Real Bill: Your Ideal Match

To fight counterfeiting, bankers are trained regarding the unique qualities of a true twenty-dollar bill. The principle is that the best way to fight counterfeiting is by being so familiar with the real thing that the slightest aberration won't fool you.

You can do the same thing when choosing a marriage partner. Instead of becoming consumed by all the things you don't want, piece together in your mind the type of person you *do* want.

Because Dennis was well into his thirties, he had begun coming to terms with possible lifelong singleness—until, that is, he met our second oldest daughter, Krissy. The romance that erupted caught our family completely by surprise. We had been thrilled with the boyfriend Krissy had been dating up until then, but something about that guy just didn't seem quite right to her. She knew exactly what she wanted: someone who was sure of himself, who had clear direction in his life, and who had a great degree of maturity. She was also looking for somebody who loved sports and with whom she could feel secure.

When Dennis came along, Krissy grabbed him. Dennis is certainly a very mature man, and as a coach, his love for sports is beyond question. He is also sure of himself and has clear direction. Just as important, he is somebody Krissy knows she can count on. She feels safe and secure in his love, and once she picked Dennis out, there was no way she was going to let him go.

I think this is a healthy way to approach the whole dating scene: having a clear picture of what you're looking for. Kevin, our oldest son, is now in his mid-twenties and thus in the thick of the dating dance. One time he had a date with a young woman whom everybody in the house referred to as "the most beautiful girl in the world." But it turns out that the most beautiful girl in the world had kissed too many guys for Kevin's liking.

Krissy's mental image helped her spot the right man; Kevin's helped him spot the wrong woman. A mental image is useful on both accounts.

The point is to know what you're looking for. Let's pause a moment and begin to build a profile of the woman (or man) you'd like to marry. It's important that you do this *before* you "fall in love" and lose all objectivity. Emotions are powerful; you need to prepare for their onslaught lest they lead you in a direction you don't want to go.

If the guy of your dreams fulfills everything on this list except, for example, he doesn't have any female siblings, I certainly wouldn't expect you to disqualify him solely on that basis. You may never find someone who fits everything on your profile, but at least you'll know what you're looking for.

The Ideal Mate

The ideal birth order to match mine is:

_____

_____

Siblings I want my future spouse to have:

_____

_____

Spiritual values I expect this person to share:

_____

_____

Material values I expect this person to share:

_____

_____

The view of children I expect this person to share:

_____

_____

Money habits I expect this person to share:

_____

_____

The type of intelligence I want this person to have:

_____

_____

The level of ambition I want this person to have:

_____

_____

The type of passion I want this person to share:

_____

_____

It Takes More Time Than You Might Think

The important thing is that you take a close look at your family, determine the dynamics that made you what you are, get a conscious grasp on what the rules in your rule book are, and then do the same for your prospective partner. *Only after you've done this will you be able to marry with confidence.*

"But Dr. Leman!" some of you might say. "That could take a long time."

You bet it can. If you want a number, here it is (some of you will yell and scream when you hear this, so get ready). *I tell couples to wait two years from the day of their first date until the day they get married.*

Why so long? The answer is twofold. First, men with bad tempers learn to hide them—for a time. Men and women with addictions can cover up their dependencies—for a season. It's a psychological fact that infatuation can bring out the best in us, so if I really want to know what a person is like, it's essential that I give enough time for that infatuation to pass. Only then will I get a good understanding of who this person really is.

Be careful you don't marry someone who could suck you dry. That's why, earlier in this book, I went into such detail about getting to know where a person is coming from. Where you're from is a good indication of where you're going. Frankly, addicts get *worse* in marriage. During the dating "dance," addicts learn to hide their tempers, abusive behaviors, and even dependency on whatever substance they are addicted to. If you don't wait until the infatuation is over, for all you know you may just be another type of high for them—but it's a high that will eventually wear off. Inevitably, they'll once again be driven by their own needs. They'll expect you to cover for them. They'll become a taker instead of a giver, and you'll run yourself ragged trying to please someone who is too self-absorbed to ever be fully pleased. (They may tell you they're pleased, but that's just a ruse because they know they're dependent on you. Their actions will speak otherwise.)

Unfortunately, negative tendencies *increase* in marriage. Controlling men tend to become even more controlling; insecure spouses tend to become even more insecure. You're living in Disneyland if you think "getting married" will solve problems like jealousy, anger, or irritability. Expect all of these issues to get *worse*, not better, once you're together in the same house.

The second reason I want couples to wait is to see if they develop what Dr. Warren calls a "companionate" love. Companionate love is a quieter, more fulfilling love that is essential to a successful marriage. It is not as hot-blooded as passionate love, yet it evolves into a high degree of caring, affection, commitment, and mutual respect. Dr. Warren has found that in about 25 percent of his clients, passionate love fails to develop into the more permanent companionate love.[4] You can't always predict how your love will develop, but you want to give it enough time to see if this deeper, quieter love evolves once the high-arousal passion has dimmed.

As a psychologist, I usually assume that there are serious, underlying issues when a couple has known each other for just a few months and yet is willing to bet the rest of their lives on marriage. Think about it: If you truly believe in lifelong marriage, why would you make a decision you will be forced to live with for the rest of your life on such flimsy evidence? The usual answer is that one or both partners have been negatively imprinted by at least one parent, which makes them want to get married hastily. Unfortunately, the same thing that moves you to get married too quickly is the same thing that will lead you to choose exactly the wrong person.

Slow down. Take your time. A potential marriage needs to be looked at from every possible angle. You've got to consider how well this person will fit into your life emotionally, intellectually, spiritually, financially, as a parent to your children, and as a son-in-law or daughter-in-law to your parents. These judgments take time.

Besides, it's not as if you're "waiting" to relate to this person. You can still do the most intimate things—like talking and appropriate kissing. The only thing you're delaying is sexual activity and living at the same address. Many couples who spend two years working on their respective issues enjoy the first year of marriage that much more because they have truly gotten to know each other, including how that person wants to be loved. Those who rush into marriage often have an extremely difficult first year, as they are still getting to know each other.

Last Borns: Put On the Brakes!

I want to add a special word of warning to all the last borns reading this chapter. It will be most difficult for you to wait. As a rule, your birth order is the most likely to rush a relationship. Unfortunately, you are also the most likely to rush out! A case in point is Trudy.

Trudy was an A-minus student in high school who could have gone to a good college. She loved drama and wanted to do some acting in college. If she couldn't make it as an actress, she figured she'd like to come back to her hometown and teach drama in the high school there.

But then Jack swept her off her feet. He was tall, good-looking, athletic, and, most important of all to last-born Trudy, he had a terrific sense of humor. To spend a day with him was like spending a day in an amusement park—one exciting moment after another.

She decided to marry him. He worked as a messenger for a local company and didn't make very much money, but she figured "things would work out." Her parents, aware that Trudy had been raised in relative affluence and had no idea about how difficult it can be to live on a substandard income, tried to talk Trudy out of the marriage. Trudy said there was nothing they could do; she was eighteen years old, she was in love, and she was going to get married.

"But Trudy," her parents pled, "think about the future. What about your plans to go to college? Jack can't afford that. And where will you live? Are you willing to stay in a studio apartment, because that's all you'll be able to afford!"

Trudy was undeterred. Jack was all she saw, and he was all she wanted.

Four days after high school graduation, Jack and Trudy were married, and Trudy went to work in a grocery store as a cashier.

The rest of the story is a sad but not uncommon history. Jack drifted from job to job, never making much more than minimum wage. His sense of humor began to grate on Trudy's nerves. He laughed about things that weren't funny anymore. Six years later Trudy was still working as a cashier. She resented having given up her dream of spending her life working in dramatics. Every time somebody put up a poster in the grocery store where she worked, announcing that season's school play, Trudy felt her heart drop out of her.

Trudy also grew tired of their small, cramped apartment. She wanted a bigger one, but there wasn't enough money, and Jack insisted on subscribing to full cable, even though the $50 a month it cost would have gone a long way toward at least getting them a one-bedroom apartment instead of a studio.

Worse, Trudy realized she didn't love Jack and probably never really had. She hadn't known the difference between love and infatuation and hadn't given the relationship time to show the difference.

Poor Trudy felt trapped.

Now, we were able to discuss some of the practical ways her life and marriage could be enlivened, but I share this story to show you just how *dangerous* it can be to rush into something without considering the long-term implications. As an eighteen-year-old, Trudy thought she couldn't survive without being Jack's wife; after just five years of living with him in a cramped, studio apartment, she could hardly stand the sight of him. Do you want to feel like your life is over when you're just twenty-three years old?

Let me add, going slowly is especially crucial for those of you contemplating a second marriage. We'll talk more about this in the "blended families" chapter.

I am not trying to turn romance into a coldly calculated and clinical task. I believe in love and romance, but I also believe in comparison shopping. One look at my waist will prove the truth of that old saying, "Kissing doesn't last, but good cooking does." Well, it's also true that romance and sexual passion may cover up birth-order incompatibilities for a while—but not forever. And since marriage will, at times, *feel* like forever, it's a good idea to think long term.

Well, now that you have the picture of what makes a good match and an image of the ideal marital partner firmly in your mind, how do you go about finding him (or her)? We'll talk about this in the next chapter.

6

Finding a Prince (or Princess) in the Swamp

'I've got some bad news for you. There are a shrinking number of "good ones" out there.

I'm referring, of course, to marital partners.

Unfortunately, our society's infatuation with breaking the rules has caught up to us. More and more, I'm seeing adults who have yet to grow up, who even at the age of thirty aren't emotionally or spiritually mature enough to even think about marriage. The sad fact is, they want to suck you into their own miserable existence. You need to learn how to watch out for them.

For starters, *you'll do yourself a big favor by realizing that upwards of 80 to 90 percent of the people out there simply aren't good enough for you*. Think that sounds harsh? It's not if you want an enriching marriage that never grows stale.

Think about it. Imagine how special a person has to be to come into your life and love you for who you are, without putting unfair demands on you or asking you to always jump higher, do more, increase your income, or make him or her happier. Most of us aren't looking for a coach. We're looking for what Billy Joel sang about when he said, "I love you just the way you are."

I'm telling you as a psychologist, the percentage of people who will truly love you "just the way you are" without trying to change you is very small, indeed.

This is particularly true for those of you who have already been married and have a few kidlets hanging around your ankles. Think of how extraordinary, how almost unworldly a man has to be to willingly take on the burden of being a father to a two-year-old and four-year-old—neither of whom are his. Sports magazines are filled with athletes who make millions while failing to pay child support *for their own children*. And in the midst of this world, you expect to find someone who will be an unselfish dad to two kids he had no hand in conceiving?

Don't get me wrong; there are a few of them out there. If a man is the second son of nine children with five younger sisters and spent a good deal of time taking care of those siblings, he might just be what God ordered in your life—but don't count on it.

Let's look at a few ways you can wade through the cultural muck and find a real prince or princess.

Choose Your Swamp Carefully

Brian and Kelly have been married for almost two years. By all accounts they seem to be a good match for each other. Brian is a first born and Kelly is the baby of the family. Everyone told them that the first two years of marriage would be hard, but both Brian and Kelly are almost apologetic when they confess it's been rather easy.

That's because they made a good match and they followed the right rules. Not only do their birth orders complement each other, but they share the same values. Furthermore, they also dated for two and a half years before getting married. What I want to focus on, however, is how they met.

The happy couple met while working as counselors at Camp Firwood, a Christian camp located in the Pacific Northwest. The year Brian and Kelly met, there were about one hundred staff members, including about thirty counselors total; four marriages were spawned in this environment in one summer.

If I regularly swim in a swamp infested by piranhas, I can hardly complain when I lose a few fingers and toes. If I want to find goldfish, I need to go where goldfish swim. If you pick up your man or woman in a bar, nightclub, or similar surroundings, you're going to find the type of person who likes to hang out in such places.

Brian and Kelly met in a positive, altruistic environment. Kelly is a registered nurse and Brian was working as a counselor. When Brian brought in a young camper who needed a scraped knee taken care of, he saw Kelly at her best—caring for others, being competent, encouraging the young. Kelly, in turn, saw Brian inspire, encourage, and teach kids how to overcome their biggest fears. As an "adventure guide," Brian helped kids become comfortable with heights and learn how to work in teams.

What makes this situation such a fertile ground for romance is that a man or a woman can watch from afar the one who has caught his or her eye. Because they work together, men and women can get to know each other without the immediate intensity of a "date." Brian was able to observe Kelly, and Kelly found herself watching Brian, without any emotional (or physical) involvement. That led to more clearheaded thinking and helped both of them make an excellent choice.

If you're finding it difficult to come across the "right" man or woman, maybe you should think twice about where you hang out. Look at your social situations and ask yourself, "Is this the type of place I want my future husband (or wife) to come to often?" Instead of hanging out at bars or nightclubs, consider volunteering your time at various charities. Find a church or synagogue and become an active member.

Meeting a future wife or husband isn't kid's play. If you act like a kid, you'll probably marry a kid. You're looking for an unusual man or woman to share your life with, so you need to look in places where unusual, caring, and mature men and women hang out.

Keep to Your Own Lily Pad

One of the things you need to decide early on is why you're dating. Are you truly looking for a marriage partner, the love of your life, or are you just out to have fun? If finding a soul mate is getting ever more important to you, you're going to have to approach your dating habits from a new perspective.

The fact is, if you're like most people, you may be sabotaging your best chance to have a meaningful marital relationship right now and *not even realize it.*

Rutgers University recently published a study that showed many people today "are involved in a mating culture that may make it more difficult to achieve this lofty goal [of a lifelong, fulfilling marriage]."[1] The researchers, David Popenoe and Barbara Dafoe Whitehead, describe the modern-day dating scene as "a culture of sex without strings and relationships without rings."

Ask yourself a serious question, one that could save you decades of heartache: "Are my dating habits setting me up for divorce and getting me accustomed to discarding relationships whenever tension arises, or are they truly helping me to find a favorable marriage partner?"

In this culture, sex on the second or third (or even first) date is far from uncommon—in fact, it's the norm. This is an increasingly dangerous dance, unlikely to produce a lasting marriage. In the Rutgers study, the young people admitted that much of their dating has nothing to do with finding a potential marriage partner. "You don't go to a club to find a wife," one young man said.

Another was far more blunt: "Club girls are trash." He's willing to have sex with "trash," but wouldn't think about marrying it.

From early sex, today's dating darlings typically advance to "shacking up," or living together without being married. The number of unmarried couples who live together in America increased by close to 1,000 percent between 1960 and 1998.[2] Whereas cohabitation before marriage was an anomaly in the early 1900s, today, over half of all marriages include some form of premarital cohabitation.

Supposedly, this living together is a form of trial marriage, a way of gathering vital information about a partner's character, but guess what? This so-called "weeding out" process actually works against the intended goal of lifelong, fulfilling marriage! Instead of pulling weeds, it plants them!

A recent Penn State study found that couples who live together before getting married have poorer communication skills when trying to solve a problem than those who didn't cohabit prior to marriage. Study coauthor Catherine Cohan suggested that cohabitants "may have less invested in the relationship, leading them not to try to develop their skills."[3]

Numerous studies have shown that cohabitation results in hurting women and men who have suffered numerous relational breakups, creating an ever-growing distrust of future relationships. Such "quasi-commitments" actually weaken the mutual dedication and perseverance that is all-important for a successful marriage. It's not too surprising, then, when Popenoe and Whitehead point out that only one-sixth of cohabiting relationships last three years, and only one in ten last five years or more. Sadly, every one of these failed, cohabiting relationships makes you a little less fit to enjoy a lifelong, satisfying marriage.

I have counseled thousands of couples, before and after marriage. Some of them have lived together before tying the knot. Others never moved in together, but spent their share of time heating up the sheets. Still others managed to stay out of bed and kept their own address until the day they got married. Without equivocation I can say that if you want a marriage that takes you from your twenties until the day you die, that fulfills you and inspires others, that results in kindred-spirit communication and soul-mate loyalty, having sex before marriage and living together before marriage will take you in the wrong direction. That's *not* the best way to find your true love.

This rise in sexual activity has made a marked difference in sexual attitudes. More and more, women are seen as playthings and objects, not people to be cared for, to serve, and to love. And women are becoming just as shallow as men in this regard, a thought trumpeted and glorified on such popular shows as HBO's *Sex and the City* and Fox's *Ally McBeal*.

In her review of a successful independent film, *In the Company of Men*, Lucy Kaylin warns that we are "living in the new age of misogyny (hatred of women), an attitude that's bubbling up like molten sludge across the land."[4] The plot of *In the Company of Men* isn't hard to figure out—but it's very hard to stomach. Two guys are frustrated with life, but even more, they're frustrated with women, so they devise a plan to get back at the opposite gender. I'll let Kaylin explain what plan they come up with.

"Chad has a plan. What if they were to find a woman— an especially vulnerable one—and romance . . . her, double-team her and really race her ego; then, when the six-week business trip is just about over, they dump [her] on her head? Really destroy her. According to Chad, no matter what indignities they suffer at the hands of women . . . in the future, they'll always have the satisfaction of having gotten over big time, just this once."

After a moment of reflection, one of the lead characters gloats, "Awright! Let's hurt somebody!" They end up choosing a lonely, deaf typist.

As much as I hate to say it, men who think like this are out there. I know, because the women they've harmed have come to me for help as they try to put their lives back together after having their hearts broken in a cruel and merciless manner.

I want to let you in on a little secret, however, the type of thing you usually don't hear outside of a counseling room. Even sexually promiscuous people know that sex outside of marriage is not the most satisfying thing to do. Wilt Chamberlain created headlines when he admitted that he had experienced sexual relations with over 20,000 women in his lifetime. Unfortunately, the press didn't report the full story. Chamberlain went on in his book to say he'd rather have made love 20,000 times with the same woman—that that would have been much better.

If you really want to find the prince in the swamp, *keep your head above water* and your body out of someone else's bed. Stay on your own lily pad. If you truly want a successful marriage, living together beforehand is about the worst preparation you could imagine. To me, the saddest thing about so much casual sex is what it tells me about how men and women today view themselves. They don't see themselves as special enough to save themselves for marriage. The mere thought is an antiquated ideal in many circles.

Well, allow me to let you in on another psychologist's secret: People want what they can't have. That's right. If you give your body to a man on the first date, he's got nothing to look forward to except "more of the same." You've sold yourself cheap.

Think about it. Once you've jumped into bed with a man, he's seen every scar, he's heard every moan, he's noticed every pimple. He doesn't have to imagine anything about you. All he has to do is *remember*. You have destroyed any sense of mystery or anticipation, plus you have made yourself a prime target of *comparison*. Suddenly, you're competing with a fantasy. Are you as skinny as Kate Moss? Are your breasts as shapely as his last girlfriend's— or the new receptionist at his office? He doesn't have to guess, he just has to close his eyes and remember.

Looking for Love in All the *Right* Places

My colleague and friend, Dr. Neil Clark Warren, a clinical psychologist, has started a service I wholeheartedly endorse. Eharmony.com was created to help individuals "find and develop a happy, successful, and loving relationship." Rather than focusing on things that don't really matter—the photos and fluff that fill so many similar sites— eharmony.com has created a matching engine built upon clinical and scientific evaluations of the important attributes that lead to successful relationships.

So often throughout this book, I've stressed the importance of using your mind instead of following your feelings, and that's what eharmony helps you to do. It's based on clinical and scientific study. Dr. Warren has established a set of traits and personality combinations that result in happy, long-term marriages.

By asking you the "hard, important questions" early on, eharmony allows you to more accurately and objectively evaluate potential matches before there is an emotional connection. You learn about a person's personality, personal interests, values and beliefs, and communication style before there is any chance of being blinded by sexual chemistry. This gives you an opportunity to compare each person to the ideal profile you developed in a previous chapter.

Just as important, eharmony works to screen out "emotionally unqualified singles," helping you to avoid those who are falling in need instead of falling in love.

Interested? The easiest way to follow up is to visit eharmony's web site: www.eharmony.com. If you don't have access to the Internet, you can contact eharmony via e-mail at usersupport@eharmony.com, call toll-free 1-800-263-6133, or write to eharmony, 300 North Lake Avenue, Suite 1111, Pasadena, CA 91101.

There are a lot of dating services that focus on exactly the wrong things. I can tell you with confidence that Dr. Warren's site majors on the majors and minors on the minors. It's the best effort I've ever seen in this regard, and it has my unqualified support.

If birth order is your interest, however, you can log on to my new web site, www.eharmony.com.

A Sober Look

As you sit on your log, catching flies and waiting for your prince (or princess) to show up, never forget that some of those prospective partners carry very painful stingers. Some of these stingers will be visible. One client of mine suffered from a severe case of herpes simplex blisters. She was wearing short shorts, so she pulled them back just a little bit to reveal the inside of her leg, on which I saw some of the grossest looking things I've ever seen. The blisters—pesky little whiteheads, filled with pus, that eventually break and itch like crazy—had spread down her thighs.

Some of you may still say, "I'm willing to live with that," but have you seriously considered the cost? I know a husband who gave his wife herpes (if you marry someone with herpes, even if you're careful, you're bound to eventually contract it), with the result that she had to have five C-sections instead of vaginal births, or else risk passing the disease on to her children.

Marriage isn't easy; under the most ideal circumstances, it's still tough. A soul-mate type marriage takes a lot of work and even more understanding. The more variables you add to the pot—different views of children, troublesome in-laws, mixed religions, differing value systems—the more probable it becomes that your passion will die.

Study your guy as he swims in his swamp. What does his swamp look like? How does he keep his apartment? How does he manage his personal affairs and pay his bills? Trust me—I've never seen a romance survive repeated and incessant phone calls and threats from collection officers.

Is your prospective spouse gainfully employed and hardworking? Does he hop from pad to pad, or does he have a sense of rootedness?

Your job isn't easy, but it's not complicated. Find someone with a *complementary* birth order and roughly the same set of values. If the two of you share a bit of passion along with these two things, you're well on your way to a very satisfying marriage. If you cheat on these values and try to pretend that they really don't matter, you'll end up deeply regretting your choice.

7

Red Flags

When I was a young man, I took a carload of friends to the beach. There were a lot of teenagers there that day, and most of them ran "doughnuts" in the sand, gunning the accelerator while they turned the car hard to the left, leaving a deep, wide circle on the beach.

All day long, my friends wanted me to do the same thing. "Come on," they pled, "just one doughnut, then we'll shut up. Just one."

Frankly, I wasn't as concerned with getting caught as I was with wrecking my dad's car. You could fit the entire breadth of my mechanical knowledge on a baby tooth, but I knew enough about alignment to guess that gunning a car in circles—full of people, no less—might not be the best way to help it drive straight down the highway the next time my old man got behind the wheel.

Finally, about 4:00 P.M., they wore me out. "Okay," I said, "but just one."

I went into the spin, did about four rotations, and came out of it just in time to see the flashing red and blue lights headed my way. We had been on the beach for eight hours and hadn't seen a single police car. In fact, my estimate is that there were approximately ten and a half million doughnuts run that day, but the only person who got caught running one was yours truly.

Unfortunately, I had a bit of a brash mouth, so when the officer came up to my car and asked, "You drive like that at home, son?" all I could think to answer was, "Of course not. There isn't any sand at home!"

My so-called friends snickered loudly, and that's all it took for the policeman to rip his ticket book out of his pocket with relish, and I was thirty-five dollars poorer for "failing to show due caution."

Sometimes you can run a red light and nothing happens. Sometimes you can speed and get away with it. Sometimes you can do doughnuts all day long in the sand and never be called to account.

But other times, you better be ready to pay the price.

The same thing is true when searching for the love of your life. Every relationship occasionally throws up a "red flag," a warning sign that something needs to be checked out a little more carefully.

Megan came to my office because she was confused about her relationship with Brian. The two had been dating for several months, and the future looked bright indeed. They had even half-seriously looked at wedding rings "just for the fun of it."

Then one night they went to see a movie Brian had been talking about for weeks. When they arrived at the theater, only to find that all the remaining shows were sold out, Brian threw an absolute fit. Megan was shocked, disgusted, and embarrassed.

"We can still watch a movie," she tried to say. "Why don't we see—" but before she could finish her sentence Brian was swearing and acting like her suggestion was the most ridiculous thing he had ever heard. The night was completely ruined.

Megan started to realize that maybe she didn't know Brian as well as she thought.

You might get away with ignoring one or two signs (though if you ignore the wrong ones, you could be headed for disaster), but it's always safest to pay particular attention to any of the red flags we're about to discuss.

Relationship to Parents

Precisely because birth order is such a big deal, you need to pay careful attention here. There are three things you want to watch out for: estrangement, a destructive relationship, or an abusive relationship. Each one leaves a deep scar that the eventual spouse will have to put up with.

I learned long ago in counseling that when a parent abuses a child, the child will eventually take out that abuse by abusing someone else. It's a psychological axiom: Somebody is going to pay for that abuse. The abused person may take it out on themselves and become anorexic or bulimic; they may opt to marry an abusive person and prove to themselves that that's what they really deserve; or they may opt to become the abuser themselves and take it out on . . . *you*.

None of these scenarios is a good one. I tell young women to watch very carefully how their boyfriend treats the key women in his life: his mother, his grandmother, and his sisters. If there is a serious problem in any one of these relationships, you should proceed with caution. If there is a problem with every one of them, turn around and run the other direction—and don't leave a forwarding address! A man's relationship with other female relatives is about as good a predictor as anything else regarding his ability to be successfully married.

If you're a guy who marries an abused woman, odds are you're going to pay for that abuse as well. You reap the havoc sown by your honey's old man. She may become desperately attached and smother you with worry and concern, or she may take out her bitterness and anger on you. In either case, you're going to pay.

The best marriages occur when women find men who are comfortable with women and enjoy being in their company. In the same way, men are happiest in their marriages when their wives like to be around men (in a healthy way). Relationships with opposite sex relatives are a big, big deal. I can't stress this enough.

Conflict Problems

Even satisfied married couples are going to fight—or at the very least disagree. How you handle conflict will be a major issue in your marriage, so you want to marry someone who knows how to "fight fair."

First borns typically enter fights with one aim—to win. They have lived their entire lives with more experience, education, strength, and responsibility than all their siblings, so they're used to winning. It's all they know. If you're dating a first born, make sure he (or she) isn't taking this too far. An overly competitive spirit gets real old, real fast.

Frequently, many middle borns and last borns are not thinking about "winning" or "losing." They want to be *understood*. Unfortunately, understanding isn't even on the radar screen of your typical first born.

Middle borns would just as soon have open heart surgery as enter a fight. If possible, they'll avoid the issue. If forced to confront a disagreement, they'll likely compromise their way through it, seeking a middle ground—even at their loss. They just want the disagreement to be over with, regardless of who wins.

The last born carries a secret trump card that she has played with great success her entire life: blame other people. Whenever there's a fight, the baby of the family just wants to make sure that everyone knows that it certainly isn't *her* fault. If this tried and true practice doesn't work, the next step may be humor. The idea is, "If I can just get everybody to laugh about it, the whole problem will go away."

Sometimes, they're right.

Whatever your birth order, learning how to handle conflict is essential to building a good relationship. The love of your life will quickly become your thorn in the flesh if you can't handle disagreements with any compassion or understanding.

Red flags in this area include:

A Violent Temper

One of the most sober analyses I've ever heard came from a friend of mine. He's done extensive work with hotheads, and he told me something I'll never forget. "Kevin, men who frequently blow their temper are like pedophiles: *they never change.*"

There are always the 1 or 2 percent who prove the exception to the rule, but don't bet your life—or your one chance for marital happiness—on a 1 percent probability. An out-of-control temper is a huge issue.

Look at it this way: While dating, this guy is trying to put his best foot forward. He knows you can walk away at any moment, so he's doing his best to cover up his faults and display his most endearing qualities. He has the added benefit of controlling the environment. You don't have young children pestering you. There isn't a lot of financial pressure. And your love is still new, fresh, and fun.

If, under these ideal conditions, a man can't control his temper, he's going to be ten times worse once he gets married. Do you want your kids to grow up with a man who yells at them, maybe even shakes them? Do you want to live in genuine fear of your husband's fury?

Temper is a big one, as it points to another damaging issue when resolving conflict: control.

Control Mongering

Temper is all about control. Tempestuous people soon learn that everybody around them freezes when they go ballistic, just like the diners in that old E. F. Hutton commercial.

I've never had a woman say, "I love the way my husband controls me," yet some willingly walk into a marriage where the man they dated was extremely controlling. Control will be an issue with most first borns and only borns, but they can learn to overcome some of their worst tendencies.

At any rate, birth order can't be used to excuse a violent temper or a controlling spirit. These faults are ultimately there by a person's choice—this man or woman has chosen to let their worst tendencies become everyday realities. My best advice is to avoid these people like you'd avoid your worst enemy—because ultimately, that's what they'll become if you marry them.

Immaturity

Yet another red flag has to do with emotional maturity: Is your boyfriend or girlfriend a girl in a woman's body, or a boy wearing a man's skin?

It was 1998, and Lance Armstrong, professional bicycle racer, was facing one of those transition times that every male goes through at least once in his life, although in this case, the causes were more severe. Lance had just survived a bout with testicular cancer. After it was discovered that the disease had spread to his lungs and brain, doctors gave him a 40 percent chance of surviving, but even that, to be honest, was optimistic. They didn't want to tell him the sad truth that he probably wouldn't live.

Somehow, Lance beat the odds and the cancer left his body, but it still hung on to his spirit. After chemotherapy and the cancer's remission, Lance went back to riding his bike, but the comeback was short-lived. He placed a very respectable 14th in the Ruta del Sol (remember, Lance shouldn't have been alive at this point, much less competing at the highest levels), but then he pulled over to the side of the road in the middle of the Paris-Nice race and told his teammates he was through with racing.

In his own words, Lance writes, "Back home in Austin, I was a bum. I played golf every day, I waterskied, I drank beer, and I lay on the sofa and channel-surfed. I went to my favorite Mexican restaurant, Chuy's, for Tex-Mex, and violated every rule of my training diet. I intended never to deprive myself again."[1]

Part of this was a normal response to surviving cancer, but it's also something I've seen many men go through, regardless. They come to a point in their lives when they just decide to give up.

Lance had met Kristin Richard (nicknamed Kik) just a month after he finished chemotherapy, and the two eventually became engaged. It was with no small measure of pain that Kik watched her future husband become a golf bum. I'll let Lance tell you how she responded.

"After several weeks of the golf, the drinking, the Mexican food, [Kristin] decided it was enough—somebody had to get through to me. One morning we were sitting outside on the patio having coffee. I put down my cup and said, 'Well, O.K., I'll see you later. It's my tee time.'

"'Lance,' Kik said, 'you need to decide something. You need to decide if you are going to retire for real and be a golf-playing, beer-drinking, Mexican-food-eating slob. If you are, that's fine. I love you, and I'll marry you anyway. But I just need to know, so I can get myself together and go back on the street and get a job to support your golfing. Just tell me.

"'But if you're not going to retire, then you need to stop eating and drinking like this and being a bum, and you need to figure it out, because you are deciding by not deciding, and that is so un-Lance. It is just not you. And I'm not quite sure who you are right now. I love you anyway, but you need to figure something out.'

"She wasn't angry as she said it," Lance goes on. "Normally, nobody could talk to me like that. But she said it almost sweetly, without fighting. Kik knew how stubborn I could be when someone tried to butt heads with me. But as she spoke to me I didn't feel attacked, or defensive, or hurt, or picked on. I just knew the honest truth when I heard it."

One week later, Lance was back on his bike, training hard. About a year later, he did something that nobody thought he could do: Within two years of beating cancer, he won the most grueling sporting event in the world, the Tour de France. One year later, he repeated that remarkable feat.

Instead of being a self-obsessed little boy, Lance was reborn into a man. His high profile as the winner of the most prestigious bike race in the world has resulted in millions of dollars worth of donations to the Lance Armstrong Foundation, which supports cancer research.

But Lance's greatest motivation, according to Kik, is their one-year-old son, Luke. "This year, there is even more encouragement to pedal fast and get home from a long day on the road," Kik wrote on her web page, "because Luke is waiting to play and snuggle with his daddy.

"It's so cute to see the joy on both their faces when sweaty Lance steps through the door, always asking, 'Where's my boy?'"[2]

Now, to be honest, had Kik talked to me, I wouldn't have encouraged her to pledge her loyalty regardless of Lance's decision. On the contrary, I would have told her to run the other way until Lance decided to grow up. She risked having a little boy watching his dad sit on the couch and drink beer until he fell asleep every night, instead of one who has inspired a world with his athletic exploits. But I admire the way she stood up to her fiancé and called out the best in him. She wanted him to stop being a boy and to start acting like a man.

Unfortunately, some guys don't want to change. Even after they're married with children, they still want to go out and shoot pool or throw darts in a bar. They are boys who turn into men, get married, and go back to being boys.

Many last-born women have the same tendency. Once they finally get the wedding ring, they may "relapse" into being the "baby" who is always cared for and treated in a special way. The husband will need to be gentle, but firm: It's time to grow up and take on adult responsibilities and attitudes.

What do you do with a spouse or boyfriend/girlfriend if you notice such a relapse? First, understand that most of us want to please our spouses, but as in all areas of life, if we're allowed to get away with something, we'll take advantage of it (especially a last born).

In all honesty, this applied to me a little bit after I got married. I was as messy as a guy could be, expecting my first-born wife to pick up for me just like my mom did. I needed to grow up, and Sande called me on it. When she made it clear that she wasn't going to put up with my sloppy, boyhood antics, I shaped up, because I really did want to please her.

Don't feel obligated to put up with boyish behavior. Christian women, in particular, can be at risk here. Some of them think it's somehow more "holy" to just watch their man relapse into boyhood and do nothing. Your true job is to confront such a man lovingly, the way Kik challenged Lance. Call him to be the man you fell in love with. Let him know you still adore him and support him, but that you hate to see him become less than the man he wants to be.

If you don't protect your backside in marriage and learn to draw some lines, most men will take advantage of you. We men have mastered the ability to play possum when the child cries at night, and we are great at running out of the room as soon as our noses pick up the hint of an impending diaper change. These little games aren't fair, and you shouldn't indulge them.

Selfishness

Another red flag has to do with a person's selfishness. Ask yourself, "Is this woman a giver or a taker?" Is this the type of person who volunteers at her church or synagogue, or who has found an elderly or disabled person to take care of, or is she "always too busy" with her own social life?

John was a classic "slap happy" guy with a dark side. Soon after he came to my office he was throwing out jokes, slapping me on the back, working hard to convince me he was a "good-time-Charlie type guy," but I've seen enough people to know there was something artificial about him. For starters, he never followed through on what we had agreed upon in counseling. Whenever he told me and his fiancée that he would do something—set aside an evening for a special discussion, for instance—he inevitably called her ten minutes after he was scheduled to arrive and came up with a rather lame excuse as to why it wouldn't work out.

It didn't take me long to realize why the woman's parents had urged this couple to see me before they got married. The man was a classic taker, a manipulative controller, but he had sweet-talked this woman into becoming engaged.

Unfortunately, his bride-to-be saw only the positive side, absolutely convinced about how happy she was going to be as this man's wife and totally oblivious to all the clues pointing out how selfish he was. He always had an excuse, of course. He missed picking his fiancée up because "a friend of his really needed to share something confidential," though he never explained why he didn't call her on her cell phone instead of letting her sit and wait for over an hour. Another time, he said he had to work late, but the guy sold cars, and I don't know too many customers who stay at the car dealership until two in the morning.

As it turns out, she married him anyway, and I have now had to walk with her through the ordeal of watching her husband participate in a series of affairs. Her husband treats her like dirt. She's super mom, does everything for him and the family while he does almost nothing except bring home a sizable paycheck. She has learned to tough it out for the sake of the kids—like a lot of people learn to do—but I can tell you that she deeply regrets her Pollyanna eyes that were so blinded to all the things she should have seen about this guy's deceptions. She always saw the best in everybody, which is an admirable trait in many circumstances, but a very dangerous one while dating.

I can't tell you how many times she has come back to me, weeping and tired, telling me, "I've had it, I've just had it; I can't put up with him anymore," but she hangs in there, the stereotypical martyr in another very sad marriage.

On the other hand, I can't tell you how much you can "bless" yourself—no other word will do, really—by marrying a "giver." I know because I married one!

I was attracted to Sande in large part because of her sweet nature and giving spirit (okay, her gorgeous face didn't escape my notice either). Sometimes she overdoes it—if a waiter served her a salmon that was still trying to swim upstream, she probably wouldn't send it back—but she brings so much joy into other people's lives.

One time, she was filling up one of our cars at the gas station when she noticed a harried young woman with three shabbily dressed kids stuffed into the back of an ancient station wagon. The woman was talking somewhat loudly, so my wife could overhear what was going on.

Sande quietly told the gas station attendant that she wanted to buy that woman a battery for her car and also pay to get it installed.

"You did *what?*" I asked her, incredulous as a last born that anybody would do something like that, but you know what? Giving has a way of becoming contagious.

Several months later I was filling up my car at a gas station when I saw a man driving an old Ford station wagon. He caught my eye because the car literally "bumped" as it rolled along. I soon found out why—the front tire was flat. The man wanted the gas station to "fix" the flat, but the mechanic on duty pointed out that the tire wasn't worth fixing. It was as bald as Michael Jordan's head.

I took a quick glance at the guy's tires and saw that the other three were dangerously slick.

When I went up to pay my gas bill, I asked the attendant how much it would cost to get four new tires put on that station wagon. Unfortunately, new tires for old Fords must be made of titanium or something, given the price that this guy quoted me. Still, following the example of my wife, I forked over the cash and paid to have this guy riding on something safe.

Sande is a classic pleaser, the first born of her family. As the baby, I was a little jerk. My mantra was "Give me, give me, give me." By nature, I think of myself more than I do of others, so I don't know that I ever would have thought of anonymously buying tires for this guy had it not been for Sande's example, but that's what a good marital choice does—the other person inspires you to become a better person. Instead of Sande dragging me down with lewd talk, broken promises, and abusive behavior, she calls out the best in me. I'm inspired by her and even challenged by her to bring out my best side.

Don't you want the same thing? If so, you better marry a "giver."

This is particularly true because you don't know the future, and marriage is a long journey. I read an article in *USA Today* many years ago that typifies the giving response. For four years, Meg Hectus of Mentor, Ohio, suffered from a superinfection that made it difficult for her to breathe. She required surgery and extensive medication. Stephen, her husband, showed his true heart during these difficult days. Meg told the reporter:

> Stephen can make me laugh on the way to the emergency room by responding to my "I don't want you to be upset if I die," with, "Meg, you're not going to die! You have a good ten, maybe fifteen years of suffering ahead of you!"
>
> He has learned to set up I.V.s, change dressings, and ready Adrenalin shots. He brings dinner—table, chairs, candles, and all—up to our bedroom for a weekend family get-together when I am too weak to come downstairs. Incredibly, he walks in smiling every evening and will rub my back for hours when I can't sleep. . . . Stephen escorts me to a wedding, and I feel glamorous and not swollen from cortisone.

Being a hero is not always easy and sometimes Stephen cries. That gives me the opportunity of comforting him for a change, and I feel needed.[3]

This couple obviously knows what love and marriage are all about, but ask yourself: If I were in Meg's condition, would my boyfriend (or girlfriend) act like Stephen? Or would he visit your hospital room, as one high-profile politician did, to discuss your divorce?

Age

The divorce rate for twenty-one- and twenty-two-year-olds is twice as high as it is for twenty-four- and twenty-five-year-olds.[4] The fact is, most nineteen- and twenty-year-olds really don't know who they are yet. They're still finding their way in the world, sometimes still trying on personalities. Very few at this age have learned to be independent (living in a college dorm with college-prepared food hardly qualifies as independent living, by the way).

Consequently, people this young really don't know what they're looking for. If you don't know yourself very well, of course you can't make a particularly good match. All the exercises I've suggested in this book require a bit of objectivity that the young frequently lack. Dr. Warren puts it this way:

Young people can't select a marriage partner very effectively if they don't know themselves well. In this society, where adolescence often lasts until the middle 20s, identity formation is incomplete until individuals have emotionally separated from their parents and discovered the details of their own uniqueness. Prior to their mid-20s, young adults haven't defined their goals and needs. They haven't had time to learn to be independent. They aren't in a good position to know the kind of person with whom they could form a meaningful lifelong attachment. They simply need more life experience.[5]

I heartily agree.

Wandering Eyes

I've counseled many women over the years who married men they knew to have wandering eyes. Some of them even put up with letting their husbands continue a subscription to *Playboy* magazine. They figured that once they had their men signed, sealed, and delivered, their husbands would stop their wandering ways.

It almost never works out that way.

If, while a man is engaged to you, you catch him ogling or flirting with other women, you better think twice about the relationship. Keep in mind, now, that I'm not talking about turning his head to see a pretty girl when she walks in the room. Just about every normal guy is going to do that! But there's a big difference between looking and leering, just as there is a cavernous difference between demurely appreciating a woman's physique and "accidentally" brushing up against her—or worse, going up and pinching her.

Through the years, I've seen the scales tip both ways. Women can be just as bad as men in this area. When I walked through a college dorm twenty or thirty years ago, I saw pictures of Farrah Fawcett on many a male student's walls, but rarely did I see the "male beefcake" that is on the walls of so many young women's dorm rooms in college these days. Sure, there might have been a cute closeup of David Cassidy's face, but even the most racy ones showed him with his shirt on (albeit unbuttoned by four or five buttons). Today I see pictures that would make Sharon Stone blush.

Two questions every person needs to ask of a potential spouse: "Does he respect me?" and "Does he respect women (or men) in general?"

Remember, you're looking for a *life* partner. You won't always be so young. When your breasts sag and your skin wrinkles, or, for men, when your hair falls out and your belly hangs over your belt, is this the kind of person who will trade you in for a "newer" model?

Several years ago, TLC, a popular female musical group, made a very successful video of a song called *Unpretty* that challenged the growing way young men now shamelessly flaunt their use of pornography. In the video, an attractive teen almost submits to the risks of breast-implant surgery to please her boyfriend, but decides against it at the last minute. When she returns home she catches her boyfriend flipping through a pornographic magazine and triumphantly snatches it out of his hands. All across the country, women have cheered in unison as they saw a woman do what they have wanted to do for so long—finally tell a man that "enough is enough."

One of the many young women the video spoke to is Kimberly Palmer, who attended Amherst College when the video came out. "TLC speaks for . . . 4 million . . . fans—young women sick of our boyfriends' reading, posting and staring at images of scantily clad women with Kate Moss hips and Pamela Anderson Lee chests," she wrote in a column for *USA Today*.

"At college," she went on, "I can't avoid images of exposed, contorted women. . . . Viewing porn used to be a clandestine activity; now, men do it openly in the co-ed common rooms of college dorms, making it much harder to ignore."[6]

A popular film, *American Pie,* depicted a supposedly "progressive" father who purchased pornography for his son to "teach him about women." Palmer writes in response to this, "It was easy for Jim's father to buy his son obscene magazines and congratulate himself for being a progressive, open-minded parent. He doesn't have to make love to his son. It's young women who have to deal with the damage inflicted by pornography. We have to try to understand why there is a stash of obscene videos under our boyfriends' beds, and somehow try to believe that they don't objectify our bodies in the same way."[7]

Women rightly view porn as a competitor and an obvious threat. Let's be honest here. Women naturally compare themselves with other women. They are always checking each other out. Just watch them. When two women watch another woman walk by, you frequently hear something like, "Look at that dress; isn't that cute?"

If you're a woman, already predisposed to compare yourself physically, you're putting yourself at high risk by getting involved with a guy who's into pornography. The research is pretty clear. Most guys who use porn before marriage may stop using it for a year or so after marriage, but the vast majority of them return to the highly provocative pictures. And then they end up in my office with the usual problems caused by heavy porn use: the selfishness that arises from a highly addictive behavior, chronic premature ejaculation, and the like.

If your guy has provocative posters and skin magazines lying around, know this: Regardless of what he says, deep down he sees you as a sexual receptacle of some sort. Do you want to be little more than a human dumping ground for his sperm?

Sexual Abuse

If you are considering marrying a potential spouse that has been sexually abused as a child, let me offer you this advice. You and your spouse must receive counseling to discuss the wide-reaching impact the abuse had on his or her life and the repercussions for your future. Do not enter into marriage without openly discussing these issues and being realistic about what it means for your marriage.

Since some of you might automatically reject this line of thinking, I want to point out that my goal is to help you have the happiest marriage possible, and I'm telling you, sexual abuse is a biggie. Many of the sexual symptoms and problems that routinely arise among people who have been abused show their face only after marriage.

I've already said this, but it is so important that it bears repeating. Throughout every date and every waking moment up until the time you get married, the man or woman you're checking out is showing you his or her best side. It'll never get better than this, in the sense that the other person will never have more motivation than they already have to treat you with care, kindness, compassion, and genuine love.

That's why you need to be quite ruthless in checking this person out. As you're dating this man, how does he treat you? Does he willingly spend time with you—outside of bed—or do you have to fight for it? Does he affirm you and make you feel special, or does he walk into your apartment, throw back a couple beers, roll around with you in the sheets, and then leave to go shoot pool with the guys?

If he's just getting off on you and continuing his male buddy system, you don't have much to lose, frankly. I know many women who think an unfaithful, untrustworthy guy is better than no guy, but I couldn't disagree with that sentiment more. A loser is stopping you from finding a keeper. You won't find a man of good character if you're constantly hanging on to a man of low character.

A red flag always points to something getting worse. If you marry a man who doesn't handle his finances well, for instance, be prepared to have your own credit go down the tubes, because your credit records will join the two of you in holy matrimony. You've got to be careful here, because sometimes a potential weakness can look like a real strength. I've had women come to me before marriage, gushing about the amount of money their boyfriends spend on them—taking them out to eat, buying them flowers, and then giving them that huge, Rock of Gibraltar engagement ring. One year later, however, they're back in my office. Suddenly, their husband's "generosity" is causing a lot of marital problems. They still haven't paid off that ring, and the creditors are lining up.

I can tell you with some degree of certainty that you should consider every weakness your current dating partner has, and ask yourself if you could live with that weakness if it doubles—because it probably will.

Do yourself a favor. Don't ignore the red flags. Go into marriage with both eyes wide open.

8

Do You Want to Feel like This for the Rest of Your Life?

Are you caught in a toxic relationship and can't find your way out? Or is your problem a little less severe—perhaps you find yourself falling into the same relational trap, over and over and over. All of us occasionally face ruts, and this is no less true of relationships than it is with any other part of being human. If you're willing to change, you might be amazed at how much difference it can make in your dating life. Ruts can really hold us down and blind us to new opportunities.

I chuckled when I read the story of George Will, a renowned ABC political analyst and nationally syndicated columnist, who for years wrote all his books with a yellow pad and a Montblanc fountain pen. He wouldn't even consider the word processors and personal computers that promised to make his task easier.

In February of 1995, while leaving the ABC studios after taping *This Week,* Will slipped and fell on a patch of ice, breaking his right arm in the process. With his writing hand out of commission for at least six weeks, Will was understandably concerned. He told Brian Lamb, who wrote *Booknotes,* "I write all the time. It's a metabolic necessity for me. . . . I love it. To me, it's more fun than anything. . . . I write on yellow tablets in my office in Georgetown, on airplanes, everywhere. I have an itch to write. I would explode if I couldn't write."[1]

What is a man who feels like he'll explode if he doesn't write but who has a cast on his writing hand going to do? Will came home from the hospital, pointed to his wife's computer, and asked her, "How do you turn that thing on?"

It wasn't long before Will was hooked. He found that he could write faster on a computer than he ever could by hand—and making corrections was ten times easier.

"Haven't filled my fountain pen since," he told Lamb.[2]

It's so like human nature for us to cling to something that isn't the best or most efficient way—it's just the way we've always done it. This same principle is particularly true when it comes to relationships. So often, we do the same old thing—because we've always done it that way—but somehow miraculously expect different results.

Let me give you two examples.

It's usually women who get themselves into this situation, but in this case, John came into my office with a familiar problem. He was born late in his mother's life, and frankly, she resented his entrance. She thought she was through with mothering small children, and John was the classic "mistake." He sensed his mother's resentment, as kids usually do, but since he knew he had nothing to do with his own conception and birth, he also grew resentful of his mom's attitude.

Not surprisingly, when girls started paying attention to John's piercing blue eyes and dusty-blond hair, he ate it up. Attention from a female was intoxicating for a young man who never got all that much affection from his mom.

Then John met Shawna, the "love of his life." She was several years older than him and immediately became the aggressor in the relationship. At first, John wasn't even all that attracted to her, but eventually he became captivated by the way she pursued him. It was enthralling, and soon the two fell "madly in love."

Unfortunately, they also fell into bed. John is a conscientious man, and the early sexual activity troubled his conscience. Shawna saw nothing wrong with what they did underneath the sheets, however.

Thus began a two-year relationship that ended at least four times, but they always came back together. Like a bad cold, John and Shawna just couldn't get rid of each other.

John realized that in many ways, Shawna was just stringing him along. To preserve her power, she sometimes treated John just like his mom had treated him—with a studied indifference. Then, just when John had had enough and was ready to call it off, Shawna would pour on the affection and win him back. It was mama cat playing with a mouse.

John grew more and more frustrated. He felt guilty. He felt cheated. He felt strung along. While he was passionately attracted to Shawna and just couldn't refuse her, he also at times felt humiliated by her. As he talked to me, he described himself almost as a spider caught in an ironclad web.

After patiently listening long enough to get the pattern, I asked John a question that has become one of my favorites: "Do you want to feel this way for the rest of your life?"

"No," John replied. "That's why I came to you."

"Well," I said, "you're going to feel this way as long as you stay with Shawna."

I could see a light click on in John's head. He thought the problem was his conflicting emotions. His real problem, frankly, was hooking up with a woman who treated him just like his mom had. It was making him miserable, and it would always make him miserable, unless he made a change.

Janice found herself in a similar predicament. In this case, she was devastated over her boyfriend's infidelity. It hurt all the more because her father had been unfaithful to her mother, and Janice saw firsthand the misery that infidelity carries in its wake.

Finally, after almost forty minutes, Janice confessed that this wasn't the first time Eric had been unfaithful. She was certain of at least one other time and suspected there was possibly yet a third.

That was all I needed to hear.

"You know how you feel right now, Janice?" I asked her.

"Yeah."

"It really hurts, doesn't it?"

"It sure does."

"If you marry Eric, you'll feel this way for the rest of your life."

What both John and Janice needed to develop is the courage to walk away from a bad relationship. As a psychologist, I need to tell you that some deep-seated character issues will never be resolved in certain people's lives. If a man is a habitual adulterer before he gets married, a piece of paper won't stop him after he gets married. If a woman is a manipulating power broker as your girlfriend, the odds are good she'll be a manipulating power broker as your wife.

Don't get me wrong. I believe all of us can change, *if we want to*. The problem is, neither Shawna nor Eric wanted to change. They pretended to want to change lest they lose their stranglehold on their current sexual partner, but both were so entrenched in their attitudes and so unaware of how evil they were acting that I knew any change of heart was simply wishful thinking.

If a dating partner is making you feel consistently miserable, ask yourself, "Do I want to feel this way for the rest of my life?"

If the answer is no, get out of the relationship! Muster up the courage to walk away. You won't find a healthy relationship while you're entrenched in an unhealthy one, for the simple reason that healthy people don't get involved with others who are already attached! Your only hope for a rewarding, satisfying, inspiring relationship is to get out of a frustrating, defeating, discouraging, and manipulating one.

Why People Stay

Basically, I've found that people stay in lousy relationships for a variety of reasons. Some people feel they don't "deserve" any better. Let me answer that one by saying all of us deserve to be treated with respect. Sure, you've made a few mistakes. You may even be a single parent, which of course means whoever marries you will be asked to take on additional parenting responsibilities. But that doesn't mean you should just accept the "leftovers." You're far better off staying single than you are settling for a less than respecting relationship.

Other people stay in a bad relationship because they fell in love with a fantasy rather than with reality, and they don't want to let that fantasy go, even though the reality has become so awful. Rather than admit they made a terrible mistake by allowing the infatuation to lead them into a disastrous relationship, they hang in there, feebly holding on to a false image. Do yourself a favor. Marriage is too serious and too long to ever let yourself be blinded by reality. Before you commit to such an intense, till-death-do-us-part relationship, you must maintain open eyes and passionately pursue the truth. None of us bats .1000. All of us are liable to pick a few bad ones now and then; don't wreck your chance for marital happiness by refusing to admit you made an earlier mistake.

Others have such a defeated self-image that they can't see themselves as ever being happy, so being in a relationship that makes them unhappy fits in with their view of life. Set yourself free. Get out of a bad relationship. Remember, there is tremendous power in the word *No*.

Know the "No" Power

I share this story in a previous book *(Making Sense of the Men in Your Life)* but I think it's just as relevant here, so allow me to quote myself!

"Dr. Leman, we'd like you to appear on a panel for us again," Oprah's associate producer inquired (very early in the morning, I might add). "Think you could get on a plane today and come out to Chicago?"

"I don't think so," I replied.

I have learned to avoid panels with a passion. You never get to fully express your perspective when five people appear at the same time, and I'm simply not interested in shouting over others to gain my thirty seconds of air time.

Forty-five minutes later, Oprah's senior producer called me. "I understand you have a problem with our associate producer and you don't want to appear on the show."

"No, that's not true," I said. "I don't have any problem with that producer."

"Well, did you know we're the top-rated talk show?"

"Sure, I know that."

"Then why did you turn us down?"

"I don't do panels," I explained.

"Oh," she said.

Twenty minutes later the senior producer called back. "We decided to change the show."

"What's the change?" I asked.

"You're it."

I was on a plane that morning.

There can be tremendous power in the word "No." "No" can move you from a terrible situation to an ideal one. But you have to be willing to suffer a "mini loss" if you want to get the real thing.[3]

Appearing on Oprah is a dream come true for many an author, but in this case the appearance was less than ideal because it would have been just a panel. Because I was willing to let something go, I found the ideal.

Do you see how you must be willing to do the same with a boyfriend or girlfriend? If you want someone who inspires you and who encourages you to become a better person, what are you doing sticking around in an unhealthy relationship that is tearing both of you down?

Remember, it's only going to get *worse* once you're married. If you're already making each other miserable, walk away while you can!

I can tell what some of you are thinking. "Dr. Leman, you make it sound so easy. I'd *like* to walk away, but I can't. It's almost like I'm addicted to this guy. What do I do?"

Well, let me give you one of my favorite prescriptions: "Cognitive Self-Discipline."

Cognitive Self-Discipline

Cognitive Self-Discipline (CSD) is for all of you who have experienced what I call the "Uh-oh" phenomenon, but you couldn't bring yourself to respond in the right way.

The "Uh-oh" phenomenon is simple. You see something in a relationship that you know isn't right, but you lack the willpower to follow it through and discover what's really going on. The reason you lack the willpower is twofold—you are likely a captive to negative parental imaging, or you are operating on your feelings.

CSD teaches people to stop, look, and listen. If you get these three steps down, you'll have mastered CSD.

CSD encourages people to use the full force of their intellect to overcome the near tyranny of their passions. I know this doesn't sound particularly romantic to some of you, but ask yourself this question: "When I've blindly followed my feelings in the past, what was the result?" If you've been negatively imprinted by a poor parental role model, odds are your feelings have led you to misery, heartache, and frustration. Do you want to feel this way for the rest of your life, or are you willing to learn a few skills that will teach you how to live differently?

Think of approaching your potential marital partner as you would an old, busy railway crossing just after you've purchased a brand-new car. That brand-new car represents your brand-new heart. You want to protect it, and to do that, you need to be cautious.

Stop

To stop means you're going to have to rise above your feelings. One of the best ways to do this, frankly, is to *stay out of bed*. I don't want to sound like a broken record, but premarital sexual intimacy has led more people into disastrous marriages than I could possibly count in my lifetime. Sex masks what is really going on in a dating relationship. Your body will betray your mind if you let it.

Instead of being carried away by passion, make a few mental notes. "What is it about this guy that is attracting me?" "Why do I find myself drawn to this woman?" As part of this analysis, you need to be aware of your weaknesses, whatever they may be: "I might be a bit starved for attention these days and easily overwhelmed by the fact that somebody actually wants to spend time with me. I need to be careful." Or this: "We always seem to have a good time, provided we end up in the sack. I wonder what a date would be like if I told him I don't want to sleep with him anymore?"

Be bold and courageous in searching out your greatest fears. If you suspect he may leave if you no longer sleep with him, try it out! Confirm or dispel your suspicions; that's what dating is for. If he hangs around, this relationship just may have a future.

Look

This will lead you into the second stage of CSD—*looking*. Be honest here. Don't do what so many women have done. "It was just a little hit, hardly a slap. He's had a tough day. That doesn't make him an abuser." Or: "Here she is jerking my chain again, but man, is she a knock-out to look at! It's worth it!"

Honestly look at this person. Compare him or her to your ideal model. There's a reason you chose a certain number of qualities you were looking for in a man or woman. Does this person (honestly, now) embody a majority of your wishes? Or are you selling yourself short?

Listen

Third, be willing to *listen*. What is your conscience telling you? Where is that "Uh-oh" coming from? Are you missing any clues or red flags? Is she too quick with a ready explanation for why everything is your fault? Is his temper really in control?

Every marriage counselor I know has experienced the same thing I have—anguished individuals confessing, "I walked down the wedding aisle knowing I probably shouldn't be doing this." These hurting souls had heard that inner "Uh-oh, be careful," but they didn't listen to it until they felt it was too late.

Besides listening to yourself, listen to some trusted others. If you can't trust your own parents, get the objective advice of wise people who love you—perhaps a clergyman, former teacher, or older sibling.

I think passion is a wonderful thing, but you can't run your life on passion; you've got to use your brain. People who aren't at such risk—that is, young adults from loving, healthy families—may be able to get by without paying so much attention to CSD. Because they've been positively imprinted, they will naturally be drawn to people who are good for them. But even in these instances we can be fooled.

Those who have suffered negative imprinting have simply got to find another way to choose relationships. You know your old method isn't working; how about trying a new one? Sure, that old fountain pen may feel comfortable, but is it truly getting you the results you desire?

The choice is up to you. You can go see a shrink for $125 a pop or you can master the principles in this book and marry a guy who's good for you.

Hungry for Abuse

I've seen enough couples get together to develop my own axiom: *People tend to marry people who reinforce their already existing self-image.* That's why it's not so surprising that daughters of alcoholics often marry alcoholics, or that daughters of unfaithful fathers tend to marry unfaithful husbands. If a woman's dad was emotionally or physically absent in her life—or if he had a tendency to be critical—this woman is probably going to be drawn to an authoritarian, controlling kind of guy. In all likelihood, he'll be considerably older than her. While she might be enamored by a fun-loving youngest born, she probably won't be drawn to him romantically (even though he would be a better fit).

In my book *What a Difference a Daddy Makes,* I make the case that a woman's self-esteem and self-perception are greatly determined by her relationship with her dad. A woman who doesn't feel good about herself actually "feels" most comfortable marrying someone who reinforces her negative self-image. She's been taught that this is how men treat women. It's the type of relationship that is most familiar to her, and therefore the one with which she is most comfortable—but this is a comfort she needs to learn how to live without.

I talked to a woman who in many ways typifies so many wounded people. She was sexually abused by her father and ended up marrying a man who abused her physically and even sexually. When she finally started to get her life turned around, she settled into a church that had a pastor who, it turns out, had raped a church member and was ultimately forced to resign.

Do you think it's an "accident" or "coincidence" that she felt so comfortable in this church, sitting under this pastor's authority? Absolutely not! She felt most comfortable with him, over all the other pastors in the area, because somehow she intuited that he was just like her dad and her husband.

If you simply follow your feelings into marriage, you're liable to perpetuate the past. Slow down, think through your decision, and make an intelligent choice. If you find yourself in a relationship that has two cups of misery for every teaspoon of happiness, ask yourself, "Do I want to feel like this for the rest of my life?"

If the answer is no, it's time to change the way you date as well as the people you date.

9

Motivational Miscues

Bad Reasons to Get Married

Money . . . sex . . . security . . . intimacy . . . loneliness . . . revenge.

People get married for all sorts of reasons. Unfortunately, if you get married for the wrong reason, you're almost certain to make the wrong choice. In this chapter, we're going to look at some of the most common motivational miscues that I've come across in my three decades of counseling couples.

This Person Reminds You of Mom or Dad

If your father is a wonderful human being and your mother has the heart of Mother Teresa, more power to you. If this person reminds you, positively, of a strong, healthy role model, by all means, go for it!

If, on the other hand, your dad did things to you that no dad should ever do to his daughter, if your mom was creative in her cruelty, if you suffered from notorious neglect, then watch out. People who have unfinished business with their parents tend to "marry" their parents in hopes of finally getting it right.

That's a prescription for disaster.

I can't tell you how many women I've seen who have been pushed around and belittled by their fathers and who promised themselves that they would *never* marry anyone even remotely close to their father, but then what happens? They find a guy who masks his control with sugar and honey. Instead of abusing her, he sweet-talks her into bed and then gives her a "really good time" (it's still abuse, but it doesn't *feel* like abuse). He controls her, but instead of using a belt, he uses roses and other bribes.

Just weeks after the marriage, the sweet flavor wears off. The previous affection and cuddling is thrown out the window in favor of immediate sexual demands. The roses mysteriously disappear as well. The guy has you now, and you'll do what he says, thank you very much.

One heartbreaking session occurred with Rita, an attractive and competent woman who married a belittling husband. Even though she admitted that Rick made her feel "stupid and worthless," Rita insisted, "I'm so lucky to have him."

I pressed her on this, asking her why she felt "so lucky" to be married to a man who made snide remarks at her expense in front of their friends (Rita was always the butt of Rick's cruel jokes).

"Well, if Rick hadn't come along, I probably never would have gotten married and had three beautiful children."

"Rita," I said, "you're attractive, intelligent, articulate, you have a good sense of humor. What in the world makes you think you never would have gotten married unless Rick had proposed to you?"

"Well . . ." I could see Rita's brain working overtime. "Who else would have me?"

Because of a forceful and critical father, Rita had almost no self-esteem; consequently, she married a man "just like dear old Dad."

Of course, negative imprinting can be far more subtle than this. Maybe your dad didn't overtly abuse you, but he also treated you as if you were "daddy's helpless little girl." Do you now find yourself hooked up with a man who wants an arm ornament and a sexual partner but not true equality as an individual? Did your mom shield you from all harm and always clean up your messes—both physical and social—and now you find yourself looking for a wife who will do the same thing?

Remember, the only good reason to get married is to share companionate love with one person for the rest of your life. Any other reason leads to frustration, bitterness, and unhappiness.

This Person Is the Opposite of Mom or Dad

"Whoa, Leman," some of you might be saying. "Aren't you talking out of both sides of your mouth? Didn't you just argue against the opposite?"

That's right, I did, but truth is often found in the middle, not in chasing two extremes.

Here's a classic case. A woman is fed up with a controlling, manipulative father, so she marries a weak man whom she is able to control. This guy's middle name is Milquetoast, and even though he's not of Italian descent, he's using a piece of spaghetti as a backbone. She's thrilled with her choice. She says "Jump!" and he asks, "How high?" He then starts jumping so frequently that his feet never touch the ground. They go to her favorite restaurants and watch the movies of her choice—no argument! They listen to her music, and she gets to decorate the apartment just the way she likes it, with no complaints.

It all seems too good to be true, and for perhaps two years or so, it is. But then reality sets in. This same guy who is Milquetoast to her is Milquetoast toward his boss, his children, and everyone else. He won't stand up for himself. Worse, he doesn't stand up for her either. She knows he hates his meat rare, but she's the one who has to tell the waiter to take it back.

In time, her accommodating husband isn't seen as polite but as weak; he's no longer nice but spineless; instead of being gentle he's childish.

Many people make the same mistake. They become so obsessed with finding a woman or a man who isn't anything like their parents, and they bend so far to avoid any similarities, that they end up becoming involved with women and men who are just as irritating as one of their parents, *only in the opposite direction*.

For example:

> If Dad or Mom was a workaholic, be careful that you're not attracted to someone just because of his fun-loving, I-don't-have-a-care-in-the-world attitude.

> If Dad was rigid, legalistic, and perfectionistic, be sure that gentleman you're attracted to has more going for him than his tendency to be a rebel.

> If Mom tended to smother you with her affection, you might have the key as to why you're so desperately attracted to a woman who seems indifferent to you.

> If your father had the backbone of Gumby, you may be attracted to someone who is forceful and authoritative, whether or not there's anything else about him that would attract you.

> If Mom or Dad were extremely religious, you may be fascinated by and drawn to someone who is openly rebellious against conventional wisdom.

Marriage is not the place to complete the parenting process—negatively or positively. It's the place to build a new family and a new home.

To Get Back at Mom or Dad—or to Show Up Your Siblings

Antoine's mom begged him, "Please don't marry her until you know her better. You've only been dating for two months and I can tell she's not your type."

Antoine was thinking, *I'm tired of other people trying to run my life. I'm going to marry her and we'll be deliriously happy together!* Besides, she was beautiful—far more attractive than any of the women who married his older brothers.

Some of you—particularly the last borns—may feel that other people have put you down and told you what to do your entire life. Your parents and your older siblings have doubted your competence, maybe made fun of you, and perhaps even told you outright that you could never, ever be as good as your older brother or sisters.

Then you find a man or woman who "shows up" your siblings by outclassing their own mates in some way— maybe they make a lot of money or are particularly attractive. You can't wait to introduce this person to your family and announce your engagement, just to see the look of envy in their eyes. You're thinking, *Just wait! I'll show them!*

As a last born myself, I don't mind this attitude—*Just wait, I'll show them*—particularly when it causes the baby of the family to do everything within his power to rise to greater heights. But it can be a disastrous line of thought when it causes you to go against what other people are telling you just to prove that they are wrong and you are right. Character inevitably shows itself; if this good-looking woman or wealthy man has poor character, eventually your siblings will pity you, not envy you. Good looks don't last forever, and money can't heal a miserable marriage.

Besides, at the risk of bursting your bubble, you need to know that your parents and siblings don't spend all day thinking about you. They have their own lives, and if you marry someone to spite them, you'll suffer for it twenty-four hours a day, all the while you may not cross their mind in any given week.

Another related problem is when a young woman marries a young man she knows her family will disapprove of, just to get back at them; or when a man marries a woman he knows holds values offensive to his family, just to state his independence.

You might think you're getting back at your parents, but in actuality you're amputating your own chance for happiness. Your parents' lives will go on. Yes, you might cause them to have a few sleepless nights, but at what cost—your own marital happiness? Eventually they'll get over it, *but you'll still be married*.

What I'm saying here is that you are not marrying for anyone but yourself. If you're marrying to show someone else up, or to prove that you're capable of getting a beautiful woman, or for any other reason except that you know and love the person you're going to marry, then you're marrying for the wrong reason and you're probably going to end up in a miserable marriage.

To Try to Rescue Someone (or Be Rescued)

Richard began dating Yvonne when he discovered that she was facing surgery for breast cancer. He had known her for a year or so, but the two had never gone out. As soon as he found out what Yvonne was facing, he began showering her with concern. He couldn't do enough for her or spend enough time with her. It wasn't long before he had told her that he loved her and she, in turn, was convinced that she was in love with him.

Richard stood by Yvonne throughout the surgery and subsequent radiation treatments. He rejoiced with her when the doctors told her that the cancer had not spread, and that there was little likelihood the cancer would ever return . . .

And then he dropped her.

Richard suffered from what I call the "White Knight Syndrome." His pattern was that he would fall all over a woman while she was experiencing problems in her life, but as soon as the temporary trouble had passed, he would realize that he wasn't really in love. Perhaps he meant to be kind, but by entering into women's lives in such vulnerable seasons, what he ended up doing was invariably cruel.

If you're a man who likes to rescue (it can go both ways, but it's more common with men), resist the urge until there is a more appropriate season to explore the potential for a lifelong relationship. You're taking advantage of a person when she is facing a crisis. What such people really need is a friend, not a love interest.

To Please Someone Else

Bill was everything Marcy's mother had hoped for her daughter: a former class president, a successful banker with political ambitions, the type of son-in-law who any woman would be proud to have. Marcy married Bill, much to her mom's pleasure, and then paid the price over the next thirty years once she realized she only *wanted* to love him but never actually did.

Never get married to please your parents. This is *your* marriage. If you are not attracted to this person, you are under no obligation to spend the rest of your life with him, just because everybody else thinks he's such a great guy.

The same holds true for your children (in the case of a second marriage). Do not get married to provide your kids with a mother or father; such marriages rarely work out. Marriage is too intimate for us to marry for any reason other than true, companionate love. Don't sell yourself short.

To Show the World You're Lovable

This is a common dating disaster, particularly among people who feel they are getting older. They're tired of showing up alone at holiday gatherings, watching their nephews and nieces, and feeling "cut out" of the conversation because they can't discuss preschool, soccer games, and the other common points of married people's discussions. Maybe you live in fear that you'll be the only one at your ten-year high school reunion who will still be single.

The temptation is to take anyone who is willing to marry you, just to show the world that you're lovable. Not only is this unfair to the person you're marrying, it's also a pretty lousy way to deal with the underlying issue of poor self-esteem.

Of course you're lovable. How can I say that without having ever met you? It's easy. If you're the type of person who is willing to read through a book like this, that tells me you're thoughtful, at least a little studious, conscientious, and probably responsible. You wouldn't have made it this far into the book without applying yourself. Mean-spirited cads who want only to manipulate and take advantage of others wouldn't dream of reading a book like this.

Getting married is not a good way to deal with low self-esteem. In fact, premature marriage is liable to make the problem worse. Marriage calls us to almost heroic sacrifice, service, unselfishness, and love. When we are still working through fundamental issues of self-image, we're not free to give to the extent that marriage calls us to give.

Deal with your self-esteem first, and then get married. For those of you who know this is a serious problem in your life, I recommend my books *When Your Best Is Not Good Enough* and *Women Who Try Too Hard*.

To Obtain Financial Security

People who marry for financial gain are making a lousy long-term investment for the sake of short-term gain. In general, women tend to be more security-minded than men (though I have seen men marry for the same reason). Sometimes, in the name of being secure, a woman will counter her heart and head and marry someone many years her senior, all for the sake of financial stability. This is particularly true if she has kids and wants them to be well provided for.

Inevitably, you will grow tired of this marriage. Essentially, you have prostituted yourself for the sake of financial gain, and you'll lose all sense of self-dignity and worth when you realize what you've done. In time, you'll decide that the cost of living without passion in a loveless marriage is too great, and your kids will be forced to go through the pain of yet another divorce.

If you're thinking that divorce is a way to get ahead financially, think again. Even for the very wealthy, your standard of living is certain to go down. After you've gotten used to certain luxuries, it will be even harder to learn how to live without them.

Fear That No One Else Will Ask

Arlene came to me as a professional real estate broker who owned her own agency. She was a successful and sweet businesswoman, who was moderately attractive.

The first time I saw Arlene, she had just passed her twenty-ninth birthday, and boy, was her biological clock ticking. She had begun dating an older, divorced guy who had one kid. The words she used to describe him were positive in nature, but almost depressing in the tone with which she uttered them: "He's such a nice guy, a hard worker, a good provider, honest, forthright . . ."

These are all admirable qualities, but whenever she spoke about this guy there was a startling lack of passion. It was almost like she was giving a class report on a former president of the United States. It became clear to me that while she admired this man, she had little passion for him and certainly didn't love him.

I looked at this attractive, funny, smart, successful, and moderately wealthy woman, wondering *Why in the world is she selling herself so short?* The bottom line was that she was pushing thirty years of age. Though she had had some shorter relationships and two steady boyfriends, there was nothing much on the horizon, and she was getting really anxious.

In an almost paternalistic fashion, I asked Arlene, "Do you really want to spend the rest of your life with this man?"

Immediately, Arlene began to cry.

"Why are you crying?" I asked.

"Because I know why you asked me that question."

"Tell me about it."

"You're asking me if I really love him."

The unspoken realization—that she didn't love him—remained unstated but clearly permeated the air.

"Are you thinking it's now or never, Arlene?"

She nodded her head.

"Arlene, listen to me. The day is going to come when Mr. Right comes into your life, and when he does, you don't want to be married to someone else." I talked to her about the "No" power, and together we discussed some of the issues that led her to have such a low view of herself.

Arlene gathered the courage to end this unfortunate relationship, and for two years she at times second-guessed her decision. After all, now she was thirty-one! But that spring, Mr. Right did indeed walk through her door. Eventually he did more than buy a house; he offered his hand in marriage, and Arlene eagerly accepted. Arlene is now happily married with two boys and the most adorable little girl you could ever imagine. Just as importantly, she truly loves her husband.

Every time I see Arlene I'm reminded: Wait. Have patience. Don't sell yourself short.

All Systems Are "Go!"

Now that we've discussed the most common motivational miscues, let's end this chapter with a look at good reasons to get married. These are qualities that you want to see in every relationship that is moving toward permanency. The difficulty with this list is that it's not enough to have three (or even four) out of five of these; at least, not if you want a successful marriage. Every one of these should be true if the relationship is worth pursuing.

I know a relationship is worthy of moving toward marriage when:

- I get excited about the thought of spending the rest of my life with this person.
- I'm willing to give 100 percent of myself to this relationship.
- I'm passionate about being with this person.
- I'd trust this person with my life.
- I have great respect for this person.
- I enjoy this person's sense of humor.

If all of these are true, you're well on your way to a satisfying union and are probably in the relationship for all the right reasons.

10

Essential Questions Most People Don't Ask

Is she beautiful?"

"Is he kind?"

"How is she in bed?"

"Does he have a good job?"

When you first start talking to people about becoming engaged, it's interesting to hear the questions they bring up. In this chapter, I'd like to ask you a few questions that you probably won't hear your friends and relatives asking you—but it's vital that you ask these questions yourself.

I love presenting marriage in a more realistic light. I remember one time I was in Alberta, Canada, talking to two thousand high school boys on the topic of sex and love. My goal was to give them as realistic a picture as I could, but first I knew I'd need to get their attention.

I'd been asked to speak to some tough audiences before, but this one looked as if it was going to be brutal. I knew the sex part of the topic would grab their attention, but I also knew they'd turn me off right away if the talk slowed down at all. A pack of teenage boys, egging each other on, could get quickly out of hand.

Several of the most important members of the school board—dignified, impeccably dressed, and obviously refined people—sat behind me on the platform. I knew that what I was about to say might make them sweat, but frankly, I was far more concerned about the audience in front of me than behind me.

"What do we call penises in our society today?" I asked.

The sea of faces before me was absolutely still. Had they heard what they thought they heard?

I was quite sure, at the same time, that I felt the heat rising on the stage behind me. Any moment I expected to hear a loud thump as the principal fainted.

But I persisted anyway.

"You heard me," I goaded them. "What do we call penises? Okay . . . what did Mom call it?"

A brave young man raised his hand. I pointed at him and he yelled out one of the more common names.

"Very good!" I turned to the chalkboard behind me and wrote the name in large letters. "What else?"

Someone shouted out another name, and this time, too, I wrote it on the board behind me. By now pandemonium had broken loose. The boys were getting into the spirit of things, exchanging high fives and slapping each other on the back as they called out the most common locker-room names for the penis. It's not every day that boys get to yell out, talking about ying yangs, weenies, tally whackers, and "the thing," not to mention the "little big man."

Once we had a good list on the chalkboard I asked the next question.

"Now . . . what about the female genitalia?"

It was suddenly deathly quiet. All conversation and laughing stopped; everyone was listening to me.

"What's the matter?" I said.

Still, no one responded.

"I know what's going on," I finally added. "You're like the guy in Denver who said to me, 'I'll tell you, but I won't tell you here.' What do you suppose he meant by that? Could it be that those names sound dirty and vulgar? Could it be that they cheapen and demean the beauty of sexual love?

"Guys, I want you to listen for a moment," I said next. "Put ten years on your life and pretend you're married. You're in bed with your spouse . . ."

Of course, at this point, the boys do a war whoop, which sounds not unlike an odd mixture of Tarzan's call and the school fight song.

Quickly I add, "and you're sleeping."

This is followed by groans, boos, and catcalls. Apparently, "in bed" and "sleeping" are not synonyms for these kids.

"All of a sudden you hear this loud croaking noise. You wake up in a fog and reach for the phone, but that's not where the sound is coming from. Then you reach for the radio, but it's not from there either. Next, you realize that scratchy noise is coming from the chest and throat of your sweetheart. She's sicker than a dog.

"'Honey, something's wrong. I think I'm sick,' she says. 'I might even throw up, but I don't think I can make it to the bathroom without your help.'

"Now you have to be up in a few hours to get ready for work, but you shake yourself awake because you know the woman you love needs you, so you crawl out of bed, take her arm, and lead her toward the bathroom."

I began to walk across the stage, acting as if someone were leaning against me.

"'Come on, hon,'" I said to the imaginary person, in my most soothing tone, "'you're going to be all right.'"

"But you know what?" There was no response to my question, but I knew they were thinking the worst. And they were right.

"You're too late. Halfway there your darling sweetheart, the love of your life, spews a four and a half footer onto the carpeted floor. She's blowing more chunks than you've ever seen in your life."

The kids are howling. "Oooooh! Groooosss!"

"And, gentlemen, guess who gets to clean it all up?"

"Oh, no!" someone yelled, "not me!"

"Oh, yes, you will," I answered. "And you know why? Because you love her. And you know what else? When you're down on your knees, scrubbing that smelly carpet, that's when you're finding out what love really is. In that moment you're coming closer to the reality of love than all the sexy movies you've seen, the filthy jokes you tell each other, and all the romantic cards you send to your girlfriends on Valentine's Day."

Having never been married, there are some aspects to a lifelong relationship that you just can't anticipate; cleaning up vomit is certainly one of them. But there are many other aspects as well, and this chapter is designed to engage you in some important questions to consider that many young couples never think to ask.

Are You Ready to Love, or Are You Captivated by Romance?

Some people make the mistake of thinking that romance is synonymous with love. It isn't. Don't be fooled into thinking that love consists of candlelight dinners, greeting cards with sentimental verses in them, or even romantic phone calls during the middle of the day. All of these things are nice, and I advise husbands and wives to do as much as they can to keep romance in their marriage—but we should never confuse these outward displays of affection with true love.

People who confuse love and romance often wind up in divorce court because they are susceptible to the dangers of romantic thinking. They may not know much about love, but they enjoy the feeling of being "in love." I admit that "being in love" feels wonderful . . . going around with a natural high, feeling lightheaded all the time, thinking that this old world is a marvelous place, that you've finally found a new purpose and zest for life. But there is a world of difference between having those feelings and loving someone. Yes, when you fall in love with someone, you will experience all of those feelings—but those feelings can also come about because you are infatuated or because of the excitement of establishing a new romantic relationship.

The love that lasts and that really matters is the kind of love that makes you get out of bed at 3:00 A.M. to tend to a sick spouse. It's the kind of love that makes you decide not to buy that motorcycle because you know your wife says you need a new dishwasher. It's the kind of love that makes you willing to watch *Monday Night Football* just because that's what your husband really wants to do.

Is this the kind of commitment you're willing to make? If not, you're not ready for marriage.

Why Am I Attracted to This Person, and Why Is He Attracted to Me?

Maybe you love to laugh, and this guy makes you laugh. Maybe you're blown away by his intellect, or maybe you feel safe around her gentle attitude. Maybe she inspires you with her dreams, or he motivates you with his discipline.

But then again, it could be that you like the way he looks—particularly when his shirt is off, he's facing away from you, and he's wearing those tight Levis. Or maybe you think she has the most beautiful face, silky hair, and the nicest pair of legs you've ever seen. If you stop to ask yourself exactly what is attracting you to this person and are forced to admit that you just like the way he or she looks, then you'd better think about walking away from the relationship—or, at the very least, postponing any thought of marriage for the time being. A mutual physical attraction is no basis for anything but the shallowest of relationships, and it is definitely nothing on which to build a lasting marriage.

In the same way of thinking, ask yourself, "Has he ever told me why he loves me?" If he hasn't, ask him and listen carefully to what he says. Does he give you shallow reasons that won't stand the test of time, or does he recognize character qualities that will never change?

One thing to watch out for—are you attracted to him because he's attracted to you? It's flattering to have someone tell you that he is in love with you, and it's only natural to wonder if anyone else will ever feel this way, but this isn't nearly a good enough reason to accept, or offer, a marriage proposal. It may sound cruel, but you are under no obligation to love someone back just because he says he's in love with you. You both deserve more than that.

Do Our Families Fit?

I always like to remind couples: *You are about to marry a person's* family. *Do you fit into that family?*

Even if your prospective spouse is estranged from his family, the fact that he is estranged is affecting him. It will affect any children you have, and it will affect the way he treats you.

Hopefully, estrangement hasn't occurred, in which case you're going to spend some of the most meaningful times of your life with that family: Christmas, Thanksgiving, Hanukkah, Passover, you name it. When someone in the family dies, you'll grieve with this group of people. When one of the younger ones gets married or graduates from college, you'll celebrate with them. If one of them gets put in prison or goes bankrupt, you'll be called on to pray with them and be a listening ear.

Are you ready for that?

Is This Person Going to Be a Good Parent to Our Children?

The next thing I remind young couples is this: *You're not just marrying a husband/wife; you're choosing your children's father/mother.* Is this woman the kind of woman you want your daughter to become? Is this man the type of man you want your son to model himself after? If not, why in the world would you get married? Most couples spend four or five years by themselves, and then the next four or five decades as parents—even though the kids will not live with them that long. Don't be shortsighted here.

Will This Person's Parents Be Good Grandparents to Our Children?

Yet another thing to realize: *You're not just choosing a father for your children; you're choosing your children's grandparents.*

Now that one of my children is married, I'm in the place where I could become a grandparent within the next nine months, so maybe I'm particularly sensitive here, but I'm telling you that grandparents often have more influence on grandchildren than you may realize. When a boy has a grandfather who's a drunk, it's naïve at best to pretend that won't affect his sense of family and heritage.

This is common sense. Who do you think gets the best start in a life? A young girl who grows up in a stable, two-parent household, with grandparents who have maintained a stable, two-parent household, and a family in which all the adults she looks up to share the same faith and the same values; or a boy who has an atheist grandmother, an agnostic father, a Baptist mother, and a grandfather that nobody wants to talk about because he's still tucked away in Sing Sing?

Grandparents certainly shouldn't be the deciding factor in your marriage. If everything else is right except for the grandparents, I'm not suggesting you dump the relationship solely on that basis. But I also believe it's foolish not to consider the larger family into which you'll be bringing your children.

Asking the Hard Questions

Let me be perfectly honest with you. Some of you are going to be afraid to ask these questions. You so want your current relationship to work that you fear putting it to the test.

Please don't make this mistake. Remember what I said in the first chapter, that probably 10 percent or less of all marriages turn out to be truly satisfying and fulfilling? That's because 90 percent of the population is willing to cut corners, ignore red flags, and run from the serious, hard questions.

The reason I wrote this book is to help you become happily married for life. It's based on my experience of talking to thousands of couples and millions of people in various formats (seminars, television, and radio). I don't want to squash your romance; I want to lead you into a soul-satisfying union with your spouse.

Muster the courage to put your relationship under the microscope. If it holds up, you can get married with confidence and joy. If it fails the test, there's still time to break off the engagement and try again.

11

Putting It All Together

Couple Power

My favorite person in all the world is Sande Leman.

Without in any way intending to boast, I sincerely wish you could enjoy what I enjoy: a rich, satisfying marriage with my best friend. If you take the above chapters to heart and put them into practice, I believe you'll be well on your way to creating such a marriage.

And when you do, you'll have the opportunity to enjoy one of the most satisfying experiences this world offers: couple power. To demonstrate the value of couple power, allow me to give you a guided tour of my own marriage—why Sande and I are such a good match, and what comes out of that.

Cub

As I've already stated, I was the baby of my family. Even though I have a doctorate, have fathered five children, am over half a century old, and have written a number of best-selling books, my family members still call me "Cub."

The last born never gets to grow up!

My oldest sibling is my sister, Sally, who preceded me by eight years. There are five years between me and my older brother, Jack.

Without a doubt, the two most influential women in my life (growing up) were my mother and my sister. Mom and I had (and still have) a great relationship. She was a registered nurse, and she worked nights. She got home just in time to kiss me good-bye, help me with my breakfast, and then she went off to bed while I was off to school.

I could talk to my mom about almost anything—and I mean *anything*. For instance, nurses use these things called "finger cots," rubber tubes that look like a condom. When I was in the seventh grade, I found my mom's stash and thought these cots were hysterically funny, so I took some to school and put on a "show" for my buddies. Of course, I was never very good about keeping things covered up at that age. Doing my laundry was always a great adventure for my mom, as I had the habit of forgetting what I left in my pockets. She especially hated it when she reached into my pockets and found something that was still alive (I loved to fish in those days and carried my bait in my pocket).

So one day my mom reached into my jeans and pulled out several finger cots. Boy, did she have a fit. The worst possible scenarios raced through her mind. As a nurse, she knew how much trouble I could be getting myself into. As soon as I got home, she sat me down, held out the cots, and said, "Cub, these aren't condoms. They won't protect you if you try to use them that way . . ."

She was very upset, on the verge of tears, terrified that her little boy was already becoming sexually active (which I wasn't).

"You mean, they won't protect me at all?" I asked her.

Putting It All Together

"No, Kevin, they won't."

"Mom, I'm really in trouble then."

I saw her lower lip tremble as I added, "I put those things on my fingers and probably shook the hands of half the people in my class today . . ."

"Kevin!"

Once she got over her near heart attack, I said, "Mom, come on! There's no way I'd sleep around like that. The only reason I took them was to have fun joking around with the guys." (Actually, I was sort of offended she thought I'd act that way.)

As you can see, Mom and I had a very open relationship. Even things like sex weren't off-limits. When I did start dating in high school, I was never afraid to bring girls home to meet Mom. There was many a high school party that was either getting boring or out of hand, and I invariably suggested to my date, "Let's go to my house."

This is not to say I grew up in *Leave It to Beaver* land. Far from it. My dad was a drinker. I don't want to dishonor him by going into details, so let's just say I saw things no young kid should ever see.

Apart from my mom, the saving grace in our home was Sally. She told me about girls, what they liked and didn't like, from the time I was eight or nine years old. It was a win-win situation. Sally could vent about all the stupid things high school boys did to her, and I could learn how *not* to behave when I got to be that age.

"Cub," she'd say, "girls don't like it when you show off, or act real cool in front of your friends, especially when you say cruel things to girls. That just makes them think you're a jerk. Your guy friends might laugh, but you'll never have a good date if you get that kind of reputation."

Sally was a great influence on my life as a kid. As captain of the cheerleaders, she made me the Williamsville High School mascot when I was just eight years old. I wore a little Billy Goat sweatshirt and had a six-inch megaphone. (I've never wanted to leave the stage since!) Sally was a great sister, helpful and encouraging. She believed in her brothers and in many ways was mama bear of the Leman cubs.

If Sande had asked me about where I got my view of women (as I've suggested you do), she would have found that both females in my family were positive examples of what a woman is supposed to be. I felt comfortable around women and respected them.

So even though my father's example was poor (some neighbor kids used to refer to the corner gin mill as my father's "office"), the influence of the rest of my family compensated. I remember during my junior year in high school, with grades that were persistently on the lower end of the alphabet (one teacher thought "F" wasn't low enough and actually wanted to give me a "Z"), the one thing that kept me going was knowing that even if I never made it above flipping hamburgers at a McDonald's, I'd still be a good husband and father.

This was said with all the Pollyannaish optimism that is typical of last borns who are always cared for, frequently spoiled, and who get away with far more than their older siblings ever did. From the time I was born, life was about having fun. In fact, I was always pushing the envelope. I remember when I was three years old, my favorite thing to do in church was to slink down beneath the pews and find women who had removed their shoes. I'd then switch the shoes with someone on the other side of the pew and wait to see what happened when eighty-year-old Mrs. Johnson tried to put on twenty-eight-year-old Mrs. Anderson's high heels.

As far as I was concerned, the rules didn't apply to me. Rules were for people like Sally, the first borns who cared about such things. My motto was clearly, "Fun at all costs."

Mr. "Push the Envelope" Meets Miss Goody Two-Shoes

Now guess who I married? Little-miss-first-born Sande! Whereas the only reason teachers hesitated to flunk me was because they couldn't imagine another nine months with me sitting in their classroom, Sande won a fourth grade essay contest on how wonderful her school was and how lovely the flowers in front of the school doors looked. From the time she dropped out of her mother's womb, Sande toed the line. She was Miss Goody Two-Shoes all the way. (Quite frankly, I think she had an enormously boring childhood.) Today, she's a Martha Stewart clone who loves to entertain and decorate, and who has even opened up her own "shabby-chic" antique shop, "Shabby Hattie."

So we got married, and guess what? Our birth orders immediately came to the fore. As an oldest born, Sande has this silly notion that you should record the checks you write in the back of the checkbook. She thinks you should know where you left the car keys. Can you believe it—she even thinks clothes should match! All of which is too taxing for my babylike mind. My system of car key management is very simple: I just leave them where I last used them. If I need to find them again, all I need to do is go back through my day and remember where I've been (although, admittedly, that's getting more and more difficult to do). As for recording checks, I just go to an ATM and ask the bank what my balance is.

Just as I was raised to be on stage (as an eight-year-old mascot), Sande was raised to be in control—which partly explains her reluctance to join me on television programs. Don't get me wrong. She's fabulous on television, but the mere thought makes her extremely nervous. It's an environment she can't control, and that threatens my lovely little first born. In fact, public speaking—which I do for a living—is Sande's worst nightmare. She was invited to speak in New York once, and they gave her about ten months lead time. Big mistake. Have you ever seen somebody spend one thousand hours preparing for a one-hour speech? My usual preparation is having dinner and asking the host what they want me to speak on. I feel very comfortable in front of large groups, and notes remind me too much of school, so I never use them.

So imagine my surprise when it's February, and I see Sande working at the kitchen table.

"What are you working on, hon?"

"My talk."

"What talk?"

"The one in New York."

"You mean the one in *November?*"

"Yeah, can you believe it? It's *only* ten months away!"

As part of her preparation, Sande started putting together a slide show, which got me a little nervous.

"Honey," I said, "I've never seen a good speaker use a slide show."

"Really," she answered. "You've never heard a good speaker."

First borns might get fearful, but they don't lack confidence.

As November drew nearer, I finally asked Sande what this talk was going to be about.

"You," she said.

"What do you mean, you?"

"I mean *you.*"

"As in *me?*"

"Of course."

Now I was getting really nervous.

Sande did an amazing job. She had our daughter Holly move the slides, showing pictures of me when I was little and saying funny things like, "I knew he had character. I just didn't realize he was such a character." Another slide brought the house down when she said, "Notice what a great dresser he was; those two-tone shoes are really nice! And the suspenders! Not to mention the hat!" It was the dorkiest picture you could imagine. Even I couldn't believe I had ever walked out of the house dressed like that.

In the end, her one thousand hours of preparation spread out over ten months really paid off. Sande got a standing ovation.

"You've really got a future," I told her, very proud of what she had done. "They gave you a standing ovation!"

"Don't be silly," she said. "I'm done. I'll never speak again."

I was awed by her success, but Sande knew what it had cost her and quickly made the decision to "retire."

All of this can be explained through our respective birth orders. Sande realizes I have a gift of getting up in front of a group and performing. She can't do that—she needs structure, carefully detailed notes, and a rigid schedule. I love to feed off a crowd, using interruptions for comic effect. One time, when speaking at a college, a student came in late, walked in front of the entire class, and sat down. His blatant actions drew the attention of everyone, so I stopped what I was doing, watching him along with the rest of the class, and after he sat down said, "Well, as I was saying, there's a one-to-one correlation between tardiness and lack of intelligence." The class roared, I made sure the student knew I was just kidding, and then I went on with the lecture.

But Sande, as a typical first born, loathes surprises. My delight is her threat. But you know what? A baby who can't keep track of things and the first born with a need to have her buttons all in a row make a very good couple. I keep Sande entertained; she balances our checkbook. One time, she spent over an hour trying to find a ten-cent discrepancy in our checkbook. I finally got so frustrated I pulled a dime out of my pocket and said, "Here, honey, I found the dime. Can we eat dinner now?"

She didn't think that was funny.

First borns need to have their angles rounded, and the baby of the family is often the best person to do it. On the other hand, babies need people who can manage the world instead of laugh their way through it.

I think we make a good match.

You may have detected that part of my initial attraction to Sande was no doubt due to my high respect for my sister, Sally. Sally the first born was to me the model of what a woman should be, and Sande fit that bill perfectly—plus, Sande's a real looker!

When you mix birth orders well, you create something that is unique to your own pairing, something I call "couple power."

Couple Power

Couple power is developed by taking two very different people who are committed to respecting each other and who believe in using their differences to complement one another rather than compete with one another. If you ever feel like you're "winning" in your marriage, I feel sorry for you. Competition creates stress, anger, and frustration. By definition, competition means that one person has to lose.

Couple power is based on encouragement, mutual respect, and cooperation. In a natural sense, two very different people make a great couple—if, that is, they are willing to take the pluses and minuses of each other and weave that psychological fabric in such a way that one partner's limitations are offset by the other partner's strengths (and vice versa).

I'm not talking about different value systems, of course. If Sande had been promiscuous when she was young, I wouldn't have been attracted to her at all. Because of my father, I certainly would have run in the opposite direction if Sande had shown any interest in alcohol. But because we shared the same values, our birth order differences made for a great match.

The key to couple power, then, is learning to use your differences. Instead of resenting these differences or always fighting about them, successful couples learn to respect each other's birth order and thus feel free to take on their own most natural roles. There's no law written anywhere that the husband has to balance the checkbook or that the wife has to do all the cooking. Sande was mortified early on in our marriage when she asked me to get an allen wrench.

"Honey, I've heard people name their boats and cars, but their tools?"

"That's not *my* name for it, that's what *everybody* calls it! Didn't your dad teach you anything?"

Well, not that, he didn't.

I know a couple in which the husband is a gourmet cook. He's fantastic in the kitchen, and his wife, well, his wife can pour a good bowl of cornflakes, but that's about it. Consequently, they decided early on that he'd always cook and the wife would do the dishes. Their two kids grew up seeing Daddy fix the meals, and Mommy cleaning up.

One day, Dad was busy doing yard work, so the mom went into the kitchen and started pulling out some pans. Their six-year-old daughter walked into the house, saw her mom, and, astonished, asked her, "Mommy! What are you doing?"

"I'm preparing dinner, sweetheart."

The little girl's eyes grew wide and she said, "I didn't know mommies can cook!"

The important thing is not *who* does something as much as the fact that everything gets done. If you were to ask my two youngest daughters whom they would prefer to have fix breakfast, I guarantee you that both of them would pick Dad. Look at your strengths and weaknesses, find out who's the most logical choice to set the family calendar, handle family finances, make sure the car gets properly maintained, and play to your strengths.

Inevitably, there is going to be a social person and a more reclusive person in any given marriage. Find a happy compromise. Somebody's going to be a decorator; somebody else is probably going to think a television set is all the decoration you need.

When I first got married, Sande had to teach me about basic things like picking up after myself. One time, she decided to go an entire week without picking up the clothes I left on the floor. By Saturday, you could walk across the room without touching the carpet. She also had to teach me that it's okay to eat more than canned peas and corn for vegetables (she also pointed out that corn is really a grain, meaning I actually liked only *one* vegetable). But Sande's healthy cooking has probably added a decade or more to my life.

Enemies of Couple Power

Many things destroy the value of couple power, including a lack of respect, the failure to "leave and cleave," unfinished daily business, and the tyranny of the urgent.

Lack of Respect

The best way to destroy couple power is by losing your respect for each other. There's nothing wrong with being a first born or a last born—it's just the way you are. You didn't choose your birth order, just as your spouse didn't choose hers. But what you must learn to do is to appreciate the strengths of your spouse's birth order. Instead of trying to make your last born behave like a responsible first born, or instead of trying to get the first born to act like a baby, play to his or her respective strengths. Provide the complementary balance.

In Christian and Jewish circles, there is a lot of talk about the "Proverbs 31" woman, an ideal wife praised by Solomon at the end of the Book of Proverbs. I think it's better to talk about the Genesis 2 woman—which, quite simply, means she's "the other half of him." We don't know which half, and frankly, the half she plays isn't nearly as important as the fact that she's playing it. Whether she's the scheduler or the social butterfly, the checkbook balancer or the spender, the cook or the breadwinner, she and her husband will have the happiest marriage when they learn to live together, complementing each other's strengths and learning to work around each other's weaknesses.

Failure to "Leave and Cleave"

The best marriage always begins with a funeral.

You read that right. It is absolutely essential that you completely leave your childhood home in order for you to build another. Leaving is about far more than residence, by the way. I'm talking about a complete psychological separation.

Why is this so important? Couple power becomes eroded when you try to turn your husband into your father. Just because your dad tuned up the car doesn't mean hubby can; conversely, just because your mom acted like an unpaid housekeeper doesn't mean your wife will happily fall into the same role.

You're starting a brand-new family, and it's time to reevaluate your assumptions. In this new family, you'll have to define new roles. You're not playing to your parents' strengths anymore; you're playing to your own strengths, as well as the strengths of your new spouse.

The best way to leave and cleave is to exchange your rule books. Get all your assumptions out in the open, *and be ready to discard any that won't fit in this new relationship*. Before you give birth to a new life together, make sure you put to death your old assumptions and expectations.

Unfinished Daily Business

Are you old enough to remember the old "ring around the collar" ads? A woman holds up a great-looking shirt, only to discover, on closer inspection, the ugly and dreaded "ring around the collar."

Any kind of residue over time will ruin something that was once spotless and clean and beautiful. That's why we go to the dentist every six months—the plaque on our teeth slowly builds up and needs to be removed. That's why our computers have a "defrag" program, to clean the computer up after a long week of work.

The same thing is needed in relationships. Every day there has to be a clearing of the air. All wrongs and slights should be placed on a short list so that things don't begin to build up. Without regular communication, couples slowly recede into a point of no return. The bitterness and anger rises to such a level that one or both partners actually turn and become an enemy of the other. They no longer seek to understand; they just want to attack.

Middle borns are the most likely of the birth orders to let this happen. They tend to hate conflict, and they think by staying silent, conflict can be avoided. Eventually, however, that shaken up can of soda pop is going to get opened, and when it does, there's going to be an explosion that'll shower everyone around them.

Wipe your slate clean every day. Make sure there aren't any hurt feelings.

The Tyranny of the Urgent

One of the primary reasons that married couples don't "wipe the slate clean" every day is that they're too busy recovering from running Susie to ballet, Jimmy to soccer, Ellen to softball, and working out at the athletic club. The next thing they know, it's 10:00 P.M., they're both tired, and it's just easier to slide into bed than to raise a topic that's really bothering them but that they know will take a good thirty minutes to discuss.

Virtually everyone who comes into my office—and I mean everyone—is living with a schedule that is packed way too tight. The net result is that we let important but nonurgent things like conversation and family bonding slide.

I thank God I'm a homebody by nature. Sande's family members were homebodies too, so we've never been "joiners." You won't find any club membership cards in our wallets, because virtually all of our activities center around our family.

It's important to get into this groove before you have kids. When I was a young married man, without children, I worked as the assistant dean of students at the University of Arizona. I remember sitting in an important meeting around an impressive oak table. All the bigwigs were there, including a vice president who talked about the fact that he was going to have to stop and see a business associate during his family's vacation.

I remember thinking, *I will never take vacation time away from my family to go do some work-related stuff.* Part of this orientation is undoubtedly the last born in me finding its way into my life, but it's something I'm very thankful for.

Good marriages take a lot of time. Raising kids takes just as much time. If you add much else to the mix (besides the requisite forty-hour workweek), something has to give, and that's usually the marriage.

Here's what this attitude has given me. As I write this, Sande and I are preparing to go off to a lake resort for four days, just the two of us. I can't wait. I have always enjoyed being with Sande more than I enjoy being with anybody else. This is far less common for husbands and wives in their fifties than you might think. Instead, people compensate for their poor marriages by becoming "married" to golf, softball, bowling, or something else, finding their satisfaction elsewhere. They dread taking vacations together because they've become strangers to each other.

In my book, finding a substitute "spouse," whether it's on a golf course or on horseback, is called "coping," not living, and I want to *live*.

How Couple Power Moves Us Forward

Two really are better than one!

John was a classic first-born "discouraged perfectionist." The discouraged perfectionist is different from the perfectionist in that he is never satisfied. Whatever he does, he always goes away thinking that he could have done it better. He is never able to settle for being number two in anything and doesn't think that merely being excellent is good enough.

John grew up trying to please a domineering father who always concentrated on the negative and never seemed to notice the good. No matter what it was—scholastic achievement, athletic performance, or any task he was trying to accomplish—John's dad always let him know he could have done it better. John's dad is an example of someone I call a "toxic parent." Some mothers and fathers really can be toxic to the healthy development of a young adult.

Like most first borns John was expected to set a sterling example for his younger brothers and sisters. He had been expected to act like an adult from the time he was just a kid. He was actually a pretty talented guy, but he was filled with feelings of insecurity and inadequacy, and you could see it by the way he stood—shoulders slouched, back slightly bent, head down. He was nearly six feet tall but looked to be about five eight or so, just because of the way he composed himself.

At least that's the way he was before he married last-born Elizabeth.

The first thing anyone noticed about Elizabeth was her laugh. She laughed all the time, but it wasn't an obtrusive, awkward, or annoying laugh. It was an infectious laugh that made everyone who heard it want to laugh right along with her. I'm sure it was that laugh that attracted John to Elizabeth in the first place.

Now, last borns make terrific salesmen, and this was certainly the case with Elizabeth. She was the sort of person who could have charmed a Republican into voting for Hillary Clinton or a Democrat into voting for Pat Robertson. When she set her immense talents to work in an effort to sell John to himself, it was only a matter of time before he came to believe in himself almost as much as she did.

For one thing, John had always been a terrible procrastinator, which is a common characteristic of a discouraged perfectionist. Because John was afraid that the end result might not be perfect, he was hesitant to get started at all. Elizabeth helped John to see that even if he did fail once or twice, it wouldn't be the end of the world—or their relationship.

Elizabeth also got John to see things that no one else could have helped him to see. Because John loved and respected Elizabeth so much, and because Elizabeth had a marvelously good-natured view about things, she enabled him to take a more realistic attitude about what others expected of him and gently helped him to lower his expectations regarding his own performance. She playfully teased him by telling him that it didn't really matter what anyone else thought of him anyway. She was the only one who mattered, and it wasn't possible for him to ever lose her love.

It's not an overstatement to say that Elizabeth performed miracles in John's life. He actually seemed to be growing taller, but it was only because he was feeling better about who and what he was. He was free, for the first time in his life, just to be himself. His self-confidence took off, his career took off, and his paychecks grew accordingly.

Someone might ask, "Well, didn't Elizabeth get anything out of the marriage? It sounds to me as if she gave and gave and gave, while John just took everything she had to offer."

My answer is that yes, at least at first, Elizabeth did the bulk of the giving, but once John came out of his shell, Elizabeth benefited greatly from John's first-born tendencies. John helped her to be more punctual. His new career achievements allowed Elizabeth to purchase and decorate the home of her dreams, while still staying home part-time (last borns never get that excited about work!).

But the more profound changes were subtler, though no less rich. Elizabeth now enjoys being married to a man with strong self-confidence. John laughs more easily and often and seems to have more energy. Gone are the depressing days when John's self-loathing and shame kept him from even trying.

In turn, now John is helping Elizabeth become a bit more organized. She could never find the type of thread she was looking for until John showed her how to set up her sewing table in such a way that everything had its place. Elizabeth was a bit absentminded and could never find her keys, so John built a key rack that he hung up just inside the closet that stands next to the front door. Sometimes Elizabeth uses that rack and when she does, she more easily finds her keys.

All in all, John and Elizabeth make a pretty terrific and now very happy team. As two different individuals with radically different histories, they have combined their strengths and gently learned from each other to overcome their weaknesses, forming the essence of couple power.

It's really exciting to see this work, as I found out after a very stressful doctor's appointment.

I Love You Just the Way You Are!

A number of years ago, I went to see a dermatologist because I was having some problems with the skin around my nose. I expected him to prescribe a lotion or a cream to "solve" my problem. Unfortunately, it wasn't nearly so simple.

"I'm afraid you have a condition called rosacea," he said.

"What's that?" I asked, and was soon sorry I had inquired when he offered the simplest explanation he could think of.

"Remember W. C. Fields? He had rosacea."

Rosacea causes the nose to become red and bulbous, and there's little doctors can do about it. That was a tough day. I do a lot of traveling and meet tens of thousands of people a year; I'm often on numerous television shows that go out to literally millions of viewers, and with all that, I didn't relish the thought of looking like an advertisement for the folks at Ringling Brothers Circus.

I could just imagine Barbara Walters talking to me on *The View*. "So, Dr. Leman, tell us about your new nose . . . I mean book! Tell us about your new book!"

That night, I explained the situation to Sande. Her reaction was perfect, and it really cheered me up. "Well, it's not really that big of a deal," she said.

"It's not?"

"No! I love you just the way you are!"

Sande could have said, "Well, don't worry—we'll go to a plastic surgeon and have it fixed," or, "That sounds awful. What will the girls think at my next high school reunion when I show up with Rudolph, the red-nosed psychologist?"

Instead, her reaction was to reassure me that her love for me wasn't dependent upon my appearance.

Here's the key: I came home a weaker person, discouraged, and a little frightened about the future. After talking with my wife, I became a stronger person, upbeat, and optimistic about our life together.

Now ask yourself, honestly, is that usually what happens when you get together with your partner? If so, you've discovered the awesome, liberating force of couple power.

If this book can help you to achieve what I already have in my own marriage, it will be worth one hundred times the cover price, quite frankly. Though I have spent a good deal of time talking about the misery of bad marriages and the angst of poor matches, few things can ever equal the joy and fulfillment of a truly good marriage, the kind you want to have.

The message of this book is quite simple. You know what kind of marriage you've dreamed about. Don't settle for less.

12

Loving the Love
of Your Life

S he just doesn't make any sense to me," Mark
complained.

"What are you talking about?"

"I shopped for two weeks for her birthday. I wanted to get her something special, but she still ended up crying on her birthday, and I don't know what I did wrong."

"What did you get her?"

"I got her two things. The first was a measuring cup."

"A measuring cup?"

"Yeah. She's always looking around for one, always losing the few she has, so I got her the mother of all measuring cups, a two-cup, super deluxe model, something she can use every day. She hates it."

"What else did you get her?"

"A fix-a-flat."

"A fix-a-flat?"

"Yeah, it's this new gizmo that you put in your car in case you get a flat tire. You spray it into the tire and it fixes the flat so you can drive to a service station. I thought she'd be touched that I was looking out for her safety, but *nooo*, I'm this awful, insensitive man."

Margaret made a similar mistake by always touching Mark's face. She touched his cheek while they were watching television or lying in bed, and to Mark these touches were incredibly annoying.

"I'm just trying to show you some affection!" Margaret explained when Mark brought up the issue.

You know what both spouses did wrong? They loved their spouse the way they wanted to be loved. Margaret likes her cheek touched, so she touches Mark's cheek. Mark doesn't like his cheek touched, so he never touches Margaret's cheek, which makes Margaret frustrated, so she touches his cheek all the more as a hint, which only bothers Mark more . . .

The same thing happened with gift-giving. Mark's favorite gift would be to receive a new power drill or handy tool. He's a practical guy who wants practical gifts. Margaret, on the other hand, is a collector. She likes to receive various sizes of glass pitchers. Mark looks at her growing collection and assumes she has more than she could ever possibly use, so he never even thinks to get her what she really wants: a new pitcher.

Love grows by degrees. Though there is a big difference between being engaged and being married (in the eyes of God and in the eyes of the government), we don't suddenly become different people the day we exchange rings, nor are we "mystically equipped" with the ability to buy appropriate gifts. We have to learn how to love each other; it's a process.

Feelings are enough to keep many engaged couples together. Your plans for the wedding, your expectations for the honeymoon, the joy of finally finding the right person, all can be pretty exciting. But the day will come, sooner than you may realize, when those feelings aren't enough. You're going to have to learn how to build a marriage day by day.

This chapter is designed to prepare you to begin loving the love of your life in the way he or she wants to be loved. Since the ability to love is a cultivated skill, I suggest you begin studying your prospective mate and *start practicing now.* Remember: Your job is not to love your spouse the way you want to be loved but to love your spouse the way your spouse wants to be loved.

The skills we've discussed for finding the right mate can also be put to good use in helping you learn how to love the right mate—and that's what this chapter is all about, helping you to discover your spouse's preferred way of being loved.

Loving the First Born

I once had a client who was an airline pilot. He could take off in New York and find his way to any airport in Europe. One of the big issues in his marriage arose when the husband grew ever more frustrated with his wife for failing to get his shirts laundered on time.

"Why doesn't he take his own laundry in?" I asked. "That should solve the problem right there."

"Because he can't find the dry cleaners!" his wife complained. "He always gets lost!"

I had to chuckle. This guy could find Frankfurt, but he couldn't find Donald's Dry Cleaning!

You know what? The sooner the wife realizes her husband will never change, the sooner she can begin focusing on loving him like he really wants to be loved. If you're married to a first born, here are a few tips.

First borns like rules, routines, and patterns. If you want to bring change to your home or marriage, you must be prepared. Feelings, frankly, won't cut it. First borns have to be convinced, but the best way to persuade them is to let them persuade themselves.

For example, let's say last-born Lisa wants a new clothes dryer. First-born Frank, her husband, is a bit tight with cash and controlling with the money flow. If Lisa really wants the dryer, her best bet is not to cry, plead, and cajole; it's to approach Frank like this:

"Frank, I had the Sears repairman come in today, and he said it would take $125 to fix our dryer, but we could buy a brand-new one for around $300. What do you think makes the most sense?"

Frank may come back with, "I don't think we have $300 right now," so Lisa needs to be prepared.

"I thought of that too. We'd have to pay $125 anyway, right, so maybe we could put that much down, if you think a new dryer is the way to go. The remaining payments would then be $30 a month for seven months. Think we could handle that?"

What Lisa is doing is letting Frank convince himself. To some of you, this might sound like manipulation. I prefer to think of it as meeting the other person where he's at. I know, I know—some of you are saying Lisa is playing into a centuries old male-superiority game, but I'm trying to be practical. My job as a psychologist is to help people deal with what *is*. I can't overturn prejudice overnight, and my experience is that if you've married a controlling man, it's highly unlikely he'll become less controlling after you're married. In other words, you're going to have to learn to live with his controlling nature.

So remember, first borns like to make decisions. They need a sense of being in control and often need a challenge to stay interested in life. Instead of telling a first born "you *look* good," try saying, "you *did* good." Recognize their accomplishments and make a big deal out of their successes.

And be prepared to follow.

Also, be realistic. This man or woman is going to spend more time at the office than you're comfortable with. Even on the weekends, they're probably going to have a conquering spirit. These are the type of folk who get up at 6:00 A.M. on Saturday to tackle the yard work. On vacation, they're likely to bring along a carefully orchestrated schedule and itinerary so that the family "doesn't miss anything."

In a classical case of confusion, I had a first-born son call a second-born brother when he heard that their two families would be on the same lake during the same week of vacation.

"Let's get our families together," the first-born brother said.

"Great," the second born responded.

"What's your schedule look like?"

"Schedule? We don't have a schedule. We're on vacation!"

There was a period of silence before the first born responded, "Okay, whatever, but we've got from two to four open on Wednesday and Friday; either of those work for you?"

If you're married to a first born, your first task may be to get him to slow down once in a while and enjoy himself, but even here, you must learn to do this in such a way that the first born doesn't feel confined or pressured.

What If You're the First Born?

If you're the first born, here are a few tips to make life easier for your spouse.

First, consistently ask yourself whether you're making marriage your number-one priority. Your biggest temptation is going to be conquering the world while ignoring your family. How much energy are you investing in other areas of your life: Your career? School? Involvement in social or civic activities? Lowering your golf handicap? Approach your marriage with the same sort of commitment you give to everything else, and you'll take a big step toward marital success.

Second, become familiar with the art of compromise. I haven't seen a successful relationship yet that didn't involve a lot of give-and-take from both parties. It isn't easy for the aggressive first born to compromise, but it can be done. Remember that things shouldn't always go your way— your spouse has friends, obligations, and desires that are just as important as yours. Fight your feelings every once in a while and be the compromiser.

Third, *talk* to your spouse, but remember that by "talking" I also mean "listening." Take time out of your busy schedule, grab a cup of coffee or go sit in the hot tub, and "reconnect" with your mate. I know how hard it is for aggressive types to do something like this, but you owe your spouse this attention. This may mean letting something "important" go undone once in a while, but so what? There's nothing more important than love.

By the way, when you talk, do your best to be non-competitive and unaggressive. Show some interest in your partner and express your pleasure at *her* achievements.

Making It with a Middle

You've got the best and worst of both worlds going for you if you've married a middle. On the positive end, several studies have shown that the divorce rate for marriages in which at least one of the partners is a middle born is much lower than for other couples. All in all, once middle borns are married, they tend to stay married. This is undoubtedly due to the middle-born's ability to negotiate and compromise. Also encouraging, middle borns are the most faithful and monogamous of all the birth orders. All of this makes the middle born a prize catch. If you are looking for someone who's going to be faithful and true, you couldn't do any better than to seek out a middle child.

On the negative side, your middle spouse will be the most secretive of all birth orders. Often feeling "left out," she has learned to fend for herself. You're going to have to really work to get a middle to open up. She may need continual assurance, and quite a bit of convincing that you really care about what she thinks. Even when she does begin to open up, she's going to be afraid of "rocking the boat," so she'll tell you what she thinks you want to hear— or just clam up about it.

Andy is a case in point. A classic middle child (older brother, younger sister), Andy married a first born, Tricia. Tricia came to me because she feared Andy was having an affair. Many symptoms were there: He stayed late at the office, wasn't talking much, seemed to be avoiding Tricia, and had lost some degree of sexual interest in her.

I sat Andy down and found, much to my relief, that there was no other woman. Instead, Andy was tired of being told what to do. Since middles don't like to make waves, Andy handled his frustration by clamming up and avoiding home, becoming more secretive. He wasn't about to confront Tricia with his frustration, but he wasn't willing to deal with it either—so he was just ignoring it, hoping it would go away.

Fortunately, Tricia as the first born took charge and decided to make a change. She set up an appointment, and the three of us began working on putting their marriage back together.

Andy was finally able to express his frustration with Tricia's perfectionism, particularly how, when she asked him to do something around the house, he felt like an idiot because it was never done "just right."

A classic case between a perfectionist first born and a mellow middle came about when Tricia asked Andy to hang a picture in their bedroom. Andy had a difficult time finding the stud. He drove a nail into the wall, but it went right in, so he pulled the nail out, moved it over two inches, and tried again.

Still, no stud.

Tricia was horrified. "Go get the stud finder! I'm sure we have one somewhere."

To be honest, Andy wasn't sure how to use a stud finder, so he kept pounding nails in, finally finding a stud on the sixth try. When he hung the picture, every hole was covered, but Tricia couldn't possibly sleep in a room that had a picture covering up such an unsightly mess, so she made a big production about getting out some wall putty, filling in the holes, and actually repainting that section to try to blend the color in.

Andy, of course, took all of this as a criticism of his inept abilities as a handyman. "I already know I'm not any good with tools," Andy confessed, "but it doesn't help that everything has to be done *just right*. And then she wonders why I put projects off for so long!"

The important thing to note here is that Tricia was burying Andy with her perfectionism, and Andy was running from Tricia with his withdrawal. Both needed to change the worst elements of their birth order and learn to come together—Tricia by being a little more encouraging and less demanding, and Andy by being a little more careful and a lot more verbal.

Typical for her birth order, Tricia took my counsel about encouraging Andy with full seriousness. We talked about ways she could build him up instead of tear him down. She discovered that leaving notes in his briefcase really meant a lot to Andy. The notes were short, but extremely effective. Tricia started encouraging Andy about everything: "Last night, after we made love, my heart kept racing for thirty minutes! I can't believe how good you are in bed. I'm still tingling, just thinking about it!"

Or this: "I know yard work isn't your favorite thing to do, but when I opened up the shades this morning and saw that you had gone ahead and done the edging like I wanted you to, well, I just want to say how much I appreciate what you've done. It looks great. Thank you! I owe you a nice, long back rub."

Tricia learned a valuable secret about being married to a middle: They shut up faster than a terrapin. Have you ever seen those turtles that we have down south? As soon as you pick them up, they pop inside their shells and close up tight. It won't take much for you to silence a middle. Don't let your middle get away with saying, "Everything's fine." Push a little bit. Ask him, "What do you mean by *fine?*"

If you're ever tempted to *not* do this, let me warn you that middles put up with being number two for only so long. Eventually they explode, and years of resentment and bitterness will take over and sometimes cause them to say very hurtful things.

Being married to a middle is like trying to keep dandelions out of your yard. One year I got lazy and let a couple comfortably nest in my lawn. Within weeks they had called all their brothers, aunts, uncles, stepparents, acquaintances, and business partners to join them. I no longer had a lawn; instead, I had to navigate through a sea of yellow.

Had I dug up that first dandelion, I would have spared myself hours of backbreaking labor, but because I let the first one in, I paid dearly as they multiplied. The same thing will be true if you're married to a middle—don't let resentments slip by undetected. Weed those suckers out!

For your own sanity, remind yourself that his reluctance to share his deepest, innermost thoughts has nothing at all to do with you. It is merely the result of his birth order and his upbringing. Focus on the positive. Being able to keep a secret is an admirable trait and can serve the middle child well in many areas of life. Any man or woman should appreciate having a spouse who doesn't feel a need to gossip or spill secrets.

Another helpful thing to do for the middle spouse is to make her feel special. Remember, middles often feel left out of the family. They're not the "responsible" one who got all the respect, nor are they the all-consuming baby who got all the laughs. Because of this it's extremely important for the middle born to be appreciated and respected by her romantic partner. The smallest gestures of appreciation, gift-giving, and thoughtfulness will go a long way with these spouses. Silence isn't golden! If you admire her understanding of a difficult subject, tell her how you feel. If her beauty takes your breath away, find the words to tell her about it. If you feel proud to be her spouse, tell others—when your spouse is listening and can overhear you.

Respect is important to a middle born. She wants it, and she needs to have it from her partner.

What If You're the Middle?

To make life go more smoothly for your spouse, practice the following ideas.

First, learn to stand up for yourself. Nobody can push you around unless you allow it to happen. I know you want everyone to be happy with you, but if you make a habit of lying down on the floor and trying to disguise yourself as a doormat, don't be surprised if your spouse walks all over you. If you learn to stand up for yourself, people will be less inclined to take advantage of you (this also holds true for first-born compliant people-pleasers, by the way).

Instead of blaming your spouse for not reading your mind, tell him what's really bothering you. I had one middle who pretended to like camping because she knew how much her husband loved it. As it turns out, her husband actually wasn't all that crazy about camping himself, but he went along because it seemed like Sharon enjoyed it so much.

Finally, after about ten years, as Sharon contemplated the thought of yet another fourteen days of swatting mosquitoes, sleeping in a tent, eating rainbow trout five days a week, and going without a shower for twice that long, she finally exploded: "Why do we always have to go to the mountains? I hate the mountains! I hate the bugs, the dirt, the smelly old fish, and picking bones out of my teeth!"

Now, as much as Sharon was angry with her husband, she should have been angry with herself for letting those emotions build up. Her husband told me he would have been more than satisfied to go to the mountains once every several years rather than every year—but Sharon never made her true thoughts known.

If you're a middle, try this: For the next date, tell your spouse what you "really" want to do. You can even put some of your compromising spirit behind it: "Honey, sometime I'd really like to go visit this new antique store that's about thirty miles away. We don't have to do it this weekend if that doesn't work with you, but sometime within the next few weeks or months could we take a drive out that way?" Remember, denying your spouse the chance to make you happy by refusing to tell him what you really want to do is probably one of the most selfish things you can do.

In fact, I'd like you to try a little exercise. I've used it with numerous clients and it really works. Write a list at the end of every day of all the things you did that you didn't have to do and that you really didn't want to do. Make up your mind to see the list grow shorter every day.

Baby's Best

Have you ever heard someone say, "My husband didn't really need a wife—he needed a mother"? If you have, chances are that person is married to a last born.

If you married "Mr. Special," the last born himself, be prepared to have fun, and make room for fun, for the rest of your life. You're going to *have* to go on occasional vacations. Your last born won't put up with staying in the same house for seasons on end without a break, so buy a suitcase and get used to reading maps.

The best thing you can do for a last born is to make his work enjoyable. The more social things become, the better he'll like them. For example, if you want to paint the house, make a party out of it. Invite your friends, get a lot of paint hats (you just know things are going to get messy), and order out some pizza.

Keep in mind, if you've married a last born, she was likely spoiled, overindulged, coddled, and treated as the special one. You see, when the baby came along, all of a sudden all the other other children in the family were seen as little adults whether they were or not. All of Mom's attention (and Dad's, too) was directed at little Emily, and in most instances the others were expected to fend for themselves.

"Mom, what's for breakfast?" asks Greg, who is six.

"Honey, there's cereal under the counter and there's milk in the refrigerator. You're a big boy now, so go ahead and help yourself."

Greg looks over and where is Emily? Cuddling in Mom's arms, feeding at her breast. Or perhaps Mom is specially preparing blended foods that Emily can digest. Either way, Emily is used to being served while Greg learns to fend for himself.

Unfortunately, as the years go by, the parents will more than likely continue doting on Emily. It's not that they love her more, but their perspective shifts. Greg will always be five-and-a-half years older than Emily, so Mom and Dad will always view Emily as the one who needs special assistance.

Adding to this effect is the fact that siblings usually cooperate with this process and even speed it along! I have seen cases where last-born children were delayed in verbal development because their older brothers and sisters did all their talking for them. "Mom, Emily needs a drink." "Mom, I think Emily is hungry."

There's also a protective element here. If a neighborhood bully starts to pick on Emily, he'll have to go through her older siblings to get at her. Is Emily having a difficult time doing her schoolwork? Well, Greg took that class five years ago and is eager to show off his learning! This goes on for one or two decades, until Emily becomes convinced that others will naturally bend their lives, schedules, and comfort around *her*.

The moment of revelation—finally viewing life as it really is—can come hard and fast for a last born once she marries. Disappointment is seen as virtual betrayal.

For example, Emily's future husband better make a big deal out of her birthday. A friend of mine made a huge mistake. He married a classic last born, and being a first born himself, he took her at her word when she said her birthday was "no big deal."

"And you believed her?" I asked, incredulously.

"Well, that's what she said!"

Hmph!

Your biggest challenge is going to be reining in the last-born's worst tendencies. When a last born sees something he wants, he doesn't add up what he'll spend on the interest payments or consider other, more important expenditures. That's the first-born's job! Instead, he whips out Mr. Visa and comes home with a big smile on his face, shocked that his spouse doesn't share his delight over his brand-new toy.

Overall, you've got to make allowance for this guy to have fun, to be the center of attention, and yet to have your respect. This is a sensitive issue, because though last borns like to be treated as "special," they don't want to be treated as inferior. You'll need to find a happy balance.

Also, be careful that you don't let the last born take advantage of you. They're born manipulators and will soon learn how to play you like Jimmy Hendrix played a guitar. Sometimes, for their own good, you're going to have to put your foot down. Sande insisted that I start picking up clothes, and I fell in line. The good news is, if you challenge us, we usually want to please you; if you don't set down some guidelines, however, we'll keep running over you until you do.

I'm not saying last borns are "devious," as much as I am saying that they have learned to be "creative." The youngest child seldom gets her way by being overpowering, so she takes advantage of her "weakness" to get her way. For example, she may tell her husband that she wants to go wherever he does for their next holiday trip—and that she wouldn't dream of imposing her wishes on him. At the same time, she lets it be known in various ways how much she misses her parents, and how it really would mean a lot to see them. What will eventually happen is that her "stronger" husband will eventually suggest that they spend the holidays with her parents, and the last-born spouse will jump up in the air as if this is the most novel—but also, absolutely, the most wonderful—idea she has ever heard, and how did he ever think of it?

For the last borns reading this, I want you to understand that I am not suggesting you are being purposefully manipulative and sneaky, but using your last-born wiles has become so much a part of your nature that you'll do it without really thinking about what you're doing. It's how you've learned to cope and relate. You have learned to make a living out of setting people up in life, and you're unusually good at reading situations and getting around people to accomplish whatever it is you want to accomplish.

Another thing you need to know about loving a last born is that he may be charming and engaging one minute, and then rebellious and angry the next. He can wake up feeling like the king of the world and come home feeling like an unemployed job seeker who has just received his fiftieth rejection.

Why does this happen? When they are children, last borns are often praised and spoiled one minute, and then laughed at and made fun of the next. Remember all that I said about the importance of family dynamics? Well, imagine that little Rosaline comes home from school with a picture of a horse she drew. She shows it to Dad who tells her it's the best horse he's ever seen, and how did he get to have such a talented little artist for a daughter. Bolstered by Dad's response, little Rosaline goes to big brother Bobby, who's feeling a little surly. Bobby takes one look at the picture and says, "You call that a horse? Looks more like a cow to me!"

Rosaline has just gone from feeling very good about herself to having her ego crushed, mashed, chewed up, and spit out.

Consequently, Rosaline goes through life with a curious dichotomy about her. She feels special, but then remembers being ridiculed by older siblings and feels insecure. Most last borns struggle with a residual feeling of inadequacy throughout their entire lives. This is seen in the smallest of details, like what name they go by. Consider the last-born comedians of our day: Eddie Murphy and Billy Crystal, for instance. Notice it's not "Ed" Murphy and "Bill" Crystal. Yet look at the credits on one of first-born Bill (notice, not "Billy") Cosby's shows and you'll see his name listed as "William," with a doctorate degree following his name.

One last thing about loving last borns: never, ever write them off. Many last borns are late bloomers. They've lived in the shadow of others for most of their lives and aren't really sure what they can do on their own. For this reason they may be a bit tentative and uncertain at first, but once they begin to gain confidence and ability, they can soar to great heights.

What If You're the Last Born?

As a last born married to a first born, allow me to give you a few juicy tidbits to make the most of your birth print while still building a positive marriage.

First, recognize that your spouse's attempt to rein in your compulsive spending and "play now, pay later" attitude is an act of love. You probably need someone to say no to you. I know you don't like the word *no*, and I realize you didn't hear it nearly as often as your older siblings did, but get used to it. You'll run your family into the ground without some degree of accountability.

Second, this is your time to learn how to serve. Now that you're a wife—and possibly, in the future, a mom—you're going to have to learn how to take care of others too. It's fine to expect that your husband will rub your feet after you come home from a long day of work—but are you willing to give him a back rub after he's spent all day doing yard work? It's going to be harder for you than any other birth order not to become self-centered. If you want a successful marriage, you need to learn how to give and be a little less selfish. Unless you realize that you get out of a relationship only what you put into it, your marriage is headed for disaster. One last-born husband confessed to me, "I know I'm selfish, but I've been that way for so long that it's hard to change."

My response to him was that he'd better change, and soon, if he wanted to save his marriage. I gave him an exercise I like to give to all last borns: At least once a month (write it on a calendar if you have to in order to remind yourself), do something for your spouse without expecting to be given anything in return. Buy him a gift, fix something she's wanted fixed, give her the day off while you watch the kids, tell him to go ahead and enjoy eighteen holes of golf. Make yourself think of ways to treat and serve your spouse.

Third, I know you love the spotlight, but remember that sometimes it's a good thing when your spouse gets to be in the spotlight too. You need to let her shine and sparkle and be the center of attention on occasion while you fade into the background.

The One and Only

You love an only child like you love Godzilla—watch out. The only child has a sense of divine right, privilege, and entitlement. If you ramble, they're probably too busy to listen; it's best to give them the "bottom line." The less sugar, the better.

The good news about onlies, however, is that they represent one of the best matches, according to the research. An only woman married to a last-born male is the ideal pairing.

With the good comes the bad, of course. At times, you may need to tell an only to "back off." Their need for control and tendency toward perfectionism has to be curtailed—not only for your sake but also for the sake of your future children.

Onlies will be most grateful if you help them accomplish their dreams. They're out to conquer the world, remember, and you might become crushed if you stand in their way. Life is about winning, and if you can help an only "win," she'll be grateful for life.

The danger, of course, is when the "winning" spirit is brought into marriage. Relationships are about trust, encouragement, commitment, and that-most-dreaded-of-words-for-an-only, compromise. Unless you have a somewhat compliant spirit, you're going to have a rough time being married to an only.

What If You're the Only?

Read the section entitled "What If You're the First Born?" and *double* its advice!

Now that we've looked at how to love each one of the birth orders in general, let's turn our attention to one of my favorite subjects: how to love your spouse in bed.

Birth Order in the Marital Bed

First Borns and Onlies

I was talking to a woman once who was married to an accountant. She went on and on about how reliable he was.

"I can always count on him. If he says he'll be there, he'll be there. If he promises to call someone or do something, he makes the call and he gets it done. Yessir, that's my Bob."

I noticed, however, a slight hesitation. While she meant to make this reliability sound like an unqualified compliment, her eyes betrayed her.

"He certainly sounds like a typical first born," I answered.

"Yes, he is. Trustworthy, reliable. He mows the lawn on Thursdays, washes the car on Saturdays. It's like clockwork."

I decided to help her out. "Let me guess. He's predictable and reliable *everywhere,* isn't he? Even in bed."

Now her eyes lit up. "Oh, is he ever. Sometimes, I really want to make love, but then I realize I know exactly what is going to happen and all the excitement vanishes. I could almost set my watch by what he does. In fact, I know he's going to approach me every five days."

She was now decidedly less upbeat and finally came out with why she wanted to talk to me in the first place. "What could be less romantic than that?" she admitted, asking, "Will he always be like this?"

I didn't tell her this, but it could have been worse. Stereotypically, you will see many a first-born controlling male who essentially demands that sex be a certain way, and he can even be forceful about it. Consequently, his partner soon feels like she is walking on eggshells or like she's auditioning for a Broadway play.

I often warn first borns, "The skill that makes you good at work is the same basic skill that works against you in your marriage—control mongering and perfectionism erode relationships rather than build them."

Don't get me wrong—we need our first borns. Computer programmers, anesthesiologists, or precision tool and dye makers rightly get rewarded and paid off for being perfect—I won't settle for "close" when it comes to anesthesia before an operation. The problem is, the guy who can spot the one cog keeping a computer program from running smoothly and receives a bonus because of it, walks in the front door at night and comments about the one thing that's out of place in the dining room, or the way his youngest daughter's hair looks, or the sweatshirt that his wife is wearing. What works at work fails miserably at home, and he unknowingly sets the rest of the evening off on a negative tone.

For all you first borns, if you want to become a passionate lover, lose the demanding attitude! If a woman feels like she's being controlled and turned into some kind of a mannequin, she's not going to respond well to your advances.

I know this because I've talked to many of your wives. I can't tell you how many women have told me that they anticipate their husbands coming home by promising themselves that "tonight will be different." They plan to give you a kiss and hug and say how glad they are that you're home as soon as you walk in the door.

Unfortunately, these good intentions get buried under years' worth of emotional baggage. As soon as the wife of a controlling man hears her husband's car door slam, everything shuts down inside her. She doesn't want it to, but she can't help it.

First-born, controlling wives do this to their husbands as well. I've seen some men almost weep at the hoops they have to jump through to get their wives naked. First, they can't even think about making love on a weeknight or weekday morning—it has to be Friday or Saturday night. The kids have to have been asleep for ninety minutes. The men have to take at least a seven-minute shower (if it's only four minutes, they'll be questioned about their hygiene—"Didn't you use a washcloth? How could you be done so soon?"), bring a towel for the wife to lie on (which reduces the area of their lovemaking to approximately eighteen by thirty inches), double-check to make sure all the children are fast asleep, turn out all the lights, and get in bed no later than 10:00 P.M. because the wife has a tendency to fall asleep rather quickly.

My wife is a wonderful lover, but early on in our marriage I, as the last born, had to learn to respect some of her first-born tendencies. Sande has what I call the "half-mile rule"—we can't make love as long as any living being is within a half-mile of our bed. As a playful last born, I could have sex while somebody was dumping a truckload of concrete outside the bedroom door!

The reason things have worked out so well for Sande and me is that we've learned to work with each other's tendencies. My wife has become more spontaneous and fun; I've learned to respect certain boundaries.

If you're the first born, you need to know how hurtful it can be to a middle born or last born—who generally doesn't share your sense of having the world's weight resting upon their shoulders—when everything becomes more important than sex. Typically, a middle- or last-born husband may come up behind you while you're working in the kitchen and begin to slyly caress you when the children aren't looking, and you say, "Not now! What are you doing?"

They think they're caressing you; you think you're being poked, groped, and choked!

If you're a first born, ask yourself, "Do I find it hard to put down the grocery list I've been working on when my husband starts nibbling the back of my neck?"

"When my wife is modeling a sexy new nightie, do I diminish her by barely looking up from my paperwork, mumbling, 'Very nice, dear'?"

You can decide to change. You can commit to yourself that the next time hubby nibbles the back of your neck, you're going to turn around and give him a kiss. The next time your wife shows you the new nightie she bought, you'll throw your papers to the floor in your haste to take her into your arms—if, that is, your marriage truly is more important to you than buying groceries or getting some extra work done at home.

An only child, particularly one who was spoiled by his parents, is likely to look at sex as an area where he gets rather than gives. In other words, he may lose patience with his wife, he won't enjoy sexual foreplay, and he's merely interested in sex because it makes him feel good. He'll *hate* it when his wife laughs, because he doesn't really connect "fun" and "sex."

Another extreme that onlies sometimes fall into is seeing sex as a form of competition. He'll try so hard to perform so well that sex becomes a chore rather than a pleasure (making him even *less* willing to hear his wife laugh in bed).

All of this can be overcome, of course, but it's helpful to know your tendencies in order to counteract them.

Last Borns

Stereotypically, last borns like to laugh in bed. They also don't mind junking a carefully prearranged schedule at the mere glimpse of a bare breast or a clean husband crawling out of a shower. So what if the husband has an 8:00 A.M. meeting—Leslie the last born is in the mood for love!

Because they were the babies in their families, last borns were probably held and kissed more than the other children and tend to be affectionate by nature. The person who reaches out and touches you on the arm when she is talking to you is likely to be a baby. I'm not saying that touching someone is a sexual act—it's not at all. But my point is that babies don't hesitate to make physical contact with other people.

Another thing about babies that we've said many times before is that they are fun-loving and adventurous. Put those two qualities together with their affectionate nature, and you'll come to the correct conclusion that the sexual aspect of marriage is of the utmost appeal to the last born.

The only drawback to this, though, is that the last born may separate what goes on in the bedroom from the other parts of his existence. He may need to learn that if he expects his mate to respond to him sexually, he had better be more attentive to her needs the rest of the time—helping with the housework, learning to pick up after himself, listening to her when she needs someone to talk to, and so on.

Middle Borns

Middles remain somewhat of a mystery, even in bed. They frequently have the toughest time feeling needed and often think of themselves as the least special, which leads to an interesting contradiction: being aggressive and competitive while also avoiding conflict. These two key components of the middle personality have never matched up in my head.

If your middle spouse is sexually frustrated, she may not tell you about it. If he wants to try something new, you may never hear him mention it—*unless you take the time to draw it out*. If you are married to a middle, please take the time to do a "sexual inventory." Middles will rarely tell you what they really want unless you pry it out of them.

Also, be especially sensitive. Middles take it more personally when they get turned down. Even for men, who are often wrongly reputed to be nothing but a walking pile of sexual desire, sex is about emotions even more than it is about physical release (at least within marriage). In two of my books, *Making Sense of the Men in Your Life* and *Sex Begins in the Kitchen,* I stress the difference between sex and sexual *fulfillment*. Sexual fulfillment meets a man's emotional needs; it requires a woman who is active, eager, initiating, and fully participating. He doesn't just want to "do you." He wants to feel respected and wanted. That's something, quite frankly, he could never get from a prostitute or any other illicit relationship.

Think *Them*

I encourage all couples to allow their partner's differences to help lead them out of their "sexual rut." First borns need to learn how to laugh with the last borns; last borns need to learn how to focus on the other; middles can gain quite a bit from learning to open up. You can't change yourself, of course, but you can occasionally step out of your normal role.

For example, if it's tough for you to be assertive, you can still learn to be assertive *once in a while*. I have little patience for clients who tell me, "I'm just not that way." Frankly, it's not a matter of what makes you feel comfortable. It's a matter of whether or not you want to meet the needs of your spouse. Because your spouse wants different things, you're going to have to learn how to exist (and even make love) outside of your own small comfort zone. Remember, a great sexual relationship is not where one person is satisfied, but two.

The key to all of this, of course, is to think *them*. Learn to put your spouse first, and focus on loving her *the way she wants to be loved*. Study your spouse, tend your marriage, pull up the weeds. I know all this takes time, but when a marriage really works, the dividends it pays are huge.

13

Finding the Love of Your Life the *Second* Time Around

Perhaps you've already been married . . . and divorced. Or perhaps you're widowed and think love may come your way once again. You've picked up this book because you're hoping to do better the second time around. I hope you won't make the same mistake Caroline made—falling into need.

Caroline is a divorced mother of two kids. Her first husband loved his golf handicap more than he loved her. Sadly, he spent more money on golf lessons than he spent on dates with Caroline, and he spent more time on the driving range than he spent with his boys. Caroline finally decided to do something about it when she found out that golfing wasn't Mark's *only* extracurricular activity.

Caroline came to me after she found herself looking forward to her oldest son's soccer games, and not just because his team was undefeated. There was a single dad—Chad—who had a son on the same team, and boy, did he seem like the kind of guy Caroline wished she had married. At first she didn't pay any attention to Chad's advances. He had a hefty belly and not much hair—not at all Caroline's type, really—but his history was similar to Caroline's. He had an unfaithful spouse who left the entire family, and now he was a single parent trying to do his best to raise good, responsible kids in a tough world. Caroline admired Chad's resolve, but even more, she craved his attention.

One Saturday Caroline realized she hadn't seen more than five minutes of the entire game. She was so engaged in conversation with Chad that she even missed her son's first goal. Two years ago, Chad never would have warranted even a second glance, but now Caroline couldn't get this guy out of her mind.

Chad finally invited Caroline out for ice cream after the game. "We'll bring all our kids, of course," he said.

The four kids (two belonging to each adult) took one booth and Caroline and Chad took the other. Before Caroline had licked the last bit of hot fudge from her sundae dish, she knew she was in love again.

Fast forward two months: Caroline had been spending all her free time with Chad and his two kids. Everybody seemed to be getting along all right, and for the first time in years Caroline realized she'd gone an entire month without feeling lonely.

Oh, it's a wonderful feeling to be loved, and man, does it get tiresome having to say good night. Inevitably, Chad took Caroline out to a really nice dinner and put a practical spin on everything. "Look, Caroline, you've got two kids and I've got two kids. Why should we both pay rent when our families are usually spending most of our time together anyway?"

Why indeed? Caroline and Chad merged the tribes and Caroline's wonderful dream became a complicated and hurtful nightmare.

The cards and presents stopped coming. Now when Chad came home from work he wanted to watch television instead of going on their usual walks. Suddenly, "I'm really tired," became Chad's most common catchphrase, a line Caroline had never heard before. Their kids started fighting with each other on a daily basis, and sometimes Caroline felt like she was in an impossible situation, trying to resolve regular disputes without being accused of playing favorites.

What happened?

Caroline and Chad thought they were falling in love, but actually they fell into need.

I've seen it happen so many times. A man is looking for someone to do his laundry and watch the kids; a younger woman with a child is looking for a new dad for her boy. These needs are buried under the first flush of romanticism. The new excitement is intoxicating, and the two lovebirds really are enthralled with each other. The needs each one feels so acutely get forgotten, but they don't go away. Instead, they wait patiently in the wings, eager for when the infatuation wanes and they can push their way into the forefront once again. That moment virtually always intersects when a couple moves in together, and the real agendas become painfully clear.

Though these needs are real, getting married is not the way to solve them. To marry for any reason other than companionate love is to court unhappiness. Caroline thought she "loved" Chad. In reality, she was lonely and grateful for his attention. Chad thought Caroline was one-of-a-kind. In reality, he was looking for someone who could help him return to a "normal" life by doing his laundry, cooking, and watching the kids. Any paid housekeeper could have done that.

No Forwarding Address Needed

Problems don't need an address. They stick to a person. You can't leave a problem behind by getting married. The pesky little things will follow you around until you deal with them.

If handling finances has been a lifelong battle for you, marrying someone with money won't solve your lack of discipline. If you eat to resolve anxiety, marrying someone who provides momentary excitement will only postpone, but not end, your issues with food. If your son misses his father, you can't find a "new" father—that man, unfortunately, is irreplaceable.

A second marriage isn't "starting over"—it's more like "adding on." I wish I could get more couples to see this. When you marry to resolve problems, you actually create more problems. Deal with the problems first. Then get married!

Numerous books have been written about "blended" families, but the title itself is a myth. Families don't blend; they collide.

The Tsunami on Tenth Street

I used to think twenty-three-year-old couples walking down the marriage aisle for the first time constituted the most naïve members of our human race.

I was wrong.

Thirty- and forty-something couples walking down the marriage aisle for the second or third time constitute the most naïve members of our human race, by far!

There are all kinds of myths about blended families. This new family will be very much like our old one (couldn't be further from the truth); love is lovelier the second time around (actually, the divorce rate is higher for repeat marriages); it's best for the kids (in fact, it makes life more difficult for the kids); it will help the children get over their loss (on the contrary, it daily reminds the kids of their loss).

If you're thinking of blending two families, my first suggestion, quite frankly, is don't do it. Raise your kids until they're adults and then at that time revisit the possibility of marriage. Bringing different kids from different husbands and wives together into a Brady Bunch marriage may make for good television, but it's the toughest thing you can do on this earth. Instead of creating a miracle on 34th Street, you're more likely to unleash a tsunami on Tenth Street.

You can't replace a kid's dad or mom, and when you try to do so, all you succeed in accomplishing is to provide a daily reminder of the dad or mom who used to be. To make things worse, now the kids will have less of their one remaining parent, because you're going to have to spend a significant amount of time on your new marriage—beginning with the honeymoon. And if the kids object, the parents invariably call them selfish!

Having said this, I know most of you will pursue a second marriage anyway. About 1,300 new blended families are formed every day in our country, and the tide shows little sign of receding.

For those of you who insist on following this course, let me give you a few tips to help make the transition go a little more smoothly (though it is still going to be plenty rough).

Go Slow

The first thing I tell people who begin this journey of dating again after being married once already is to go five times as slow as you think you need to. Rebound marriages are notorious for breaking this rule and invariably end up making a bad situation even worse. A wife or husband may suddenly feel extremely insecure and jump at the first person willing to marry them—it's sort of like saying to your ex-spouse, "See, somebody wants me!"

Make sure you're the one who really wants this person. It'll be little solace for you if your ex-spouse sees you run off into another loveless marriage. If you skip corners, ignore red flags, and rush headlong into a new marriage, you may bring even more misery into your life. Don't do this to yourself.

Keep Your Pants On

Second, keep your pants on. As an adult who was once sexually active on a regular basis, you're more likely to fall into bed because it seems more natural. For years, sexual excitement led to sexual fulfillment, and when you've been rejected or have suffered a great loss and then somebody starts touching you and your body warms up and you can't believe how good it feels, the moral brakes tend not to work so well.

Make up your mind ahead of time that you will not get involved sexually, for all the reasons I've already discussed in this book. Then, take the next step and make this commitment very clear to your dating partner: "I like you, but I will not have sex with anyone until I am married to that person. If you have a problem with that, let's get it out in the open right now, because I'm not going to change."

Saying this up front will save both of you a lot of time and heartache. I want to be honest with you—many single men aren't looking for a marital partner, even though they say they are. They're looking for a sexual outlet. The most charming guys can be the most deceitful. The only way you can tell them apart is to withhold any sexual involvement and see if so-called Mr. Wonderful still hangs around.

Keep It Quiet

Third, don't introduce your honey to your kids. They've already suffered one loss; don't needlessly lead them through another one. Meet your date outside your home during your lunch hour or some other time when the kids are already engaged so as not to infringe on their time.

"But Dr. Leman, when do I introduce them?" That's easy: Introduce your kids to your future spouse when you have a ring on your finger and a date set at the church. Only when you know the marriage is absolutely going to happen should you begin to let the bonding process take place.

Get a New House to Go with Your New Mate

Fourth, when you get married, don't move into his house; don't move into her house either. You need to live at an entirely new residence for both of you. Think about it. If you have a high view of marriage, do you really want to continue sleeping with your new wife on a bed and in a room in which you had sex with your previous wife? Not to mention the problems you'll eventually face when the kids who previously lived in that house tell the "new" kids, "This isn't your house." (I promise you, that'll happen.)

It's simply not fair to your children to allow them to see your new wife sleeping in their mother's bed, or to watch that new wife take down the previous wife's decorations and put up her own. It's cruel, it's unwise, and there's no need for it. Get a new house.

Be Patient

It takes from three to seven years for an average "blend" to take place, though it's my contention that due to birth order and other considerations, the families will never truly blend. This means that not only will you and your new spouse have to overcome everything you couldn't overcome in your first marriage, but now you'll also have to be patient as you add the very difficult task of getting kids to blend as well.

If you truly want to make this work, your bar of expectations for the first few years needs to be very low. There won't be as much time as you'd like to build intimacy as a couple. You'll have more tension than a couple starting out without kids. Occasionally, you'll disagree on child rearing and what should be done with the children, plus you'll have to step around the minefield of responding to your spouse's children's behavior.

Quite frankly, if you don't go into this thing shoulder to shoulder, committed to each other and willing to pay the price, the situation will soon bury you.

Solve Problems before the Marriage

This is such a basic thing, but as a counselor I've found it's the most basic of things that so frequently get overlooked. Especially in a second marriage, you need to learn how to solve problems that will inevitably arise *before you get married*.

Here's how you do this. Sit down with your wife-to-be and say, "All right, we're getting married in October. The first big holiday will be in November. How are we going to spend Thanksgiving?"

Watch your future wife's eyes light up as she says, "Oh, we always go to my mother's house in Boston. It's a tradition."

"I can live with that," you say. "But what about Thanksgiving next year?"

"On the other years, we'll celebrate Thanksgiving at my sister's house, just outside of Boston. Our kids get along so well, they really look forward to it."

"Let me get this straight," you say. "We're going to spend every Thanksgiving at either your mom's or your sister's house?"

Now, if you don't have any close family members, this may not be a problem. On the other hand, if you like to see your own family during these holidays, you better find out ahead of time if there's any wiggle room to this formula.

There are other things to discuss. What are you going to do if one parent has put away $25,000 for college expenses, and the other parent doesn't have anything put away? Will that money be shared, or will the one child get to go to college while the other doesn't?

Where will you vacation? What will be the new sleeping arrangements? How are you going to juggle visitation rights with the ex-spouses? How will you approach discipline?

Each one of these questions represents a potentially devastating disagreement. Face them before you've purchased a new home and signed on for a second till-death-do-you-part agreement.

The key here is to *anticipate* any possible point of contention and try to solve it before the stakes are too high. If you do this, your first year will go much easier than most.

For more on this subject, I recommend my video series titled *Bringing Peace and Harmony to the Blended Family.* I've also written a book titled *Living in a Step-Family without Getting Stepped On.*

Eyes Wide Open

Sandra's first mistake was moving into Mike's home. Mike had a bachelor pad, and Sandra immediately started "improving" it—except that Mike's two kids (Sandra had none of her own) didn't consider the changes improvements.

To get back on the kids' good side, Sandra carefully researched each child's favorite dinners. With an attitude that would have made Pollyanna blush, she eagerly announced what the family would have for dinner that night. No surprise to me, but catching Sandra completely offguard, each child ended up eating dinner at a friend's house that night, so Sandra and Mike had their fill of macaroni and cheese.

Sandra and Mike got along great, but Sandra's relationship with the children threatened to undo the couple's young marriage. When Mike's youngest daughter went out of her way to chide and harass Sandra, Mike made things worse by being overprotective of his daughter instead of standing up for Sandra.

"You're an adult," he explained to Sandra. "You should be able to understand what's going on. She's hurting over losing her mother, after all."

Every marriage goes through certain stages, particularly the first three: expectation, reality, and disillusionment. If you're trying to blend families, expect to arrive rather quickly at the disillusionment stage. It could happen in weeks rather than months.

If you go into this relationship with your eyes wide open, you may be able to avoid the other, more dangerous stages: license (because my needs aren't being met and I am disillusioned I can go and do my own thing) and separation/divorce.

There's yet a final stage, however, one that is unusually rewarding, uplifting, encouraging, inspiring, and fulfilling. I call it graceful love. This is the type of love that upholds couple power, a love that is flexible, forgiving, and encouraging. It's the type of love that colors each day with a quiet but deep joy. It may not be as flashy as infatuation; it may not send your heart racing as fast as a first kiss—but it's oh so much more satisfying.

Hold out for the best.

Epilogue

There's a scene in the movie *Titanic* that just makes me cringe. After the Kate Winslet character (Rose) becomes sexually involved with the Leonardo DiCaprio character, they rush up to the top deck of the ship. They've known each other for mere hours, and yet Winslet gushes, "When we get back, I want to go away with you!"

DiCaprio responds, "But Rose, that doesn't make any sense."

Rose then says the words that lead to disaster, almost as devastating as the iceberg that was up ahead: "I know. That's why I trust it."

Rose is living entirely off her feelings. She says she trusts her feelings precisely because they don't make any sense. She is flush with romantic infatuation, fueled by sexual hunger, and in real life, that's a sure prescription for making a decision that will lead to a miserable marriage.

My desire for you is simple. I want you to enjoy a life-long, happy, fulfilled, and satisfying marriage. The principles outlined in this book have taken much of the guesswork out of it. I do not believe there is "only one" person created just for you. Rather than pursue some hidden destiny, I think you'll increase your chances for marital success far more when you listen to your brain instead of your heart and carefully apply the lessons we've learned. Your marriage choice should "make sense."

Let's go over these principles one last time.

First, because of your birth order, there is a certain group of men and women with whom you are most likely to "fit." There is another group with whom you will probably never mesh very well. You want to find someone with an opposing birth order, ideally, someone who also had siblings of the same gender as you. Remember, there are exceptions, but you need to carefully think through these exceptions so that you understand and can logically explain why you are the way you are and why your potential spouse is the way he or she is—and why both of you would make a good fit.

Next, real intimacy isn't found in bed. Sex can actually destroy any chance you have of building a truly intimate relationship. The closeness you desire comes mostly from talking, so take the time to answer the questions discussed in chapter 3, going back through your respective childhoods to discover who each other really is. Exchange your rule books. Really get to know each other and make sure this is a good fit.

As you consider how well the two of you match up, remember that in some areas, opposites attract. Not only should you find someone with an opposing birth order, for instance, but you also want someone who has different vices. Having said that, perhaps you'll also remember that there are many things you should hold in common— your spiritual and material values, as well as your level of ambition and your depth of passion.

If you haven't yet come across anyone who seems even remotely suitable for you, consider changing the place where you look. Make a commitment to stay out of bed and start spending more time in places where you'd like your future wife or husband to be. Drop the nightclubs and bars, and check out some service opportunities.

As you look, keep your eyes open for red flags. Be careful if you discern a rocky relationship with your love's parents. Be aware of conflict problems, including a violent temper or a controlling personality. Character deficiencies such as immaturity, selfishness, and wandering eyes should give you pause.

If you find yourself in a bad relationship, garner the courage to get out of it. Learn the power in using the word *no,* and where you find it difficult to overcome negative imprinting, practice cognitive self-discipline (stop, look, and listen).

In the midst of this dating dance, do a gut-check on yourself. What are your real reasons for pursuing this relationship? You shouldn't date anyone as a mere reaction to your parents—either to please them or to get away from them. Don't get enmeshed in a rescue operation or the pursuit of wealth. And don't sell yourself short, marrying someone simply because you're afraid no one else will ask. Ask yourself the tough questions: Am I ready to love? Why am I attracted to this person? Why is he attracted to me? Do our families fit?

If you take the time to be this thoughtful, you'll have a good chance of experiencing that blessed state: "Couple Power." A good match and a good fit really can make a couple ten times stronger than two individuals. You'll enjoy a fulfilling relationship and be a model for generations to come.

Happy hunting!

Notes

Chapter 1: How My Life Changed outside the Men's Room

1. Reprinted from *Parents Apart Parents Handbook,* "Divorce in America," www.divorcenter.org

2. *Divorce Magazine,* www.divorcemag.com

Chapter 5: Find Someone Who *Is* Compatible with You

1. Harvey Araton, "Isn't There Anyone Listening?" *The New York Times,* 23 December 1999.

2. Neil Clark Warren, *Finding the Love of Your Life* (Colorado Springs: Focus on the Family Publishing, 1992), 38.

3. Ibid., 58.

4. Ibid., 92.

Chapter 6: Finding a Prince (or Princess) in the Swamp

1. David Popenoe and Barbara Dafoe Whitehead, "Sex without Strings, Relationships without Rings," The National Marriage Project, www.marriage.Rutgers.edu

2. Ibid., 19.

3. Karen Peterson, "Cohabiters May Miscommunicate," *USA Today,* 18 July 2000, 8D.

4. Lucy Kaylin, "No More Mr. Nice Guy," *GQ,* September 1997, 256.

Chapter 7: Red Flags

1. Lance Armstrong with Sally Jenkins, *It's Not about the Bike* (New York: Putnam and Sons, 2000), cited in "Tour De Lance," *Vanity Fair,* June 2000.

2. Quoted in Sal Ruibal, "Armstrong's Tour of Duty," *USA Today,* 30 June 2000, 2C.

3. "A Special Kind of Love," *USA Today,* 23 December 1986.

4. Warren, *Finding the Love of Your Life,* 11.

5. Ibid., 12.

6. Kimberly Palmer, "Male Students Flaunt Pornography," *USA Today,* 19 October 1999, 17A.

7. Ibid.

Chapter 8: Do You Want to Feel like This for the Rest of Your Life?

1. Brian Lamb, *Booknotes* (New York: Random House, 1997), 172.

2. Ibid., xxii.

3. Kevin Leman, *Making Sense of the Men in Your Life* (Nashville: Thomas Nelson, 2001), 232.

Founder of www.matchwise.com, internationally known Christian psychologist, award-winning author, radio and television personality, and speaker, **Dr. Kevin Leman** has ministered to and entertained audiences worldwide with his wit and common sense psychology.

Best-selling author Dr. Leman has made house calls for *Focus on the Family* with Dr. James Dobson as well as numerous radio and television programs including *Oprah, Live with Regis and Kelly, CBS' The Early Show, Today,* and *The View.* Dr. Leman is a frequent contributor to *CNN's American Morning.* He has served as a consulting family psychologist to *Good Morning America.*

Dr. Leman is founder and president of Couples of Promise, an organization designed and committed to helping couples remain happily married.

Dr. Leman's professional affiliations include the American Psychological Association, American Federation of Radio and Television Artists, National Register of Health Services Providers in Psychology, and the North American Society of Adlerian Psychology.

Dr. Leman attended North Park College. He received his bachelor's degree in psychology from the University of Arizona, where he later earned his masters and doctorate degrees. Originally from Williamsville, New York, he and his wife, Sande, live in Tucson. They have five children and one grandchild.

For information regarding speaking availability, business consultations, or seminars, please contact Dr. Leman at:

Dr. Kevin Leman
P.O. Box 35370
Tucson, AZ 85740
Phone: (520) 797-3830
Fax: (520) 797-3809
Web sites: www.realfamilies.com
             www.matchwise.com